The New Book of
FAVORITE BREADS
from
ROSE LANE
FARM

by
Ada Lou Roberts

Drawings by Edward J. Roberts

Dover Publications, Inc.
New York

Published in Canada by General Publishing Company,
Ltd., 30 Lesmill Road, Don Mills, Toronto, Ontario.
Published in the United Kingdom by Constable and Com-
pany, Ltd., 10 Orange Street, London WC2H 7EG.

This Dover edition, first published in 1981, is an unabridged
and unaltered republication of the work originally published
by Hearthside Press, Great Neck, N.Y., in 1960 and revised
and enlarged in 1970.

International Standard Book Number: 0-486-24091-6
Library of Congress Catalog Card Number: 80-69247

Manufactured in the United States of America
Dover Publications, Inc.
180 Varick Street
New York, N.Y. 10014

Dedication

To all those people, living and dead, who wrote
all the cook books from which I gained the ideas
that made this collection of recipes possible.

Appreciation

Grateful thanks to my son Edward, who enjoys sketching as I enjoy baking, for taking time from his busy schedule of teaching and studying to draw these illustrations of which I am so proud.

THE STAFF OF LIFE

Be careful when you touch bread.
Let it not lie uncared for—unwanted.
So often bread is taken for granted.
There is so much beauty in bread;
    Beauty of sun and soil,
    Beauty of patient toil—
Winds and rain have caressed it,
Christ often blessed it.
Be gentle when you touch bread.
            (Author unknown)

THE DRAWINGS

The sketches used throughout are not intended to illustrate recipes, but rather to show what variety can be had with a piece of dough, a pair of willing hands, and a little imagination.

INTRODUCTION

This book is not for you, unless you belong to that dedicated group of people who love to get their hands into a batch of dough and who look upon a perfect golden-crusted loaf as a work of art. A person who bakes bread because he enjoys it counts that time needed for perfect results well spent and looks for no short cuts or streamlined methods. Speed rarely brings out the best in a loaf of bread. I have instituted no short cuts, as such, in my mixing procedure. It is true that the use of a yeast improver and the method of adding ingredients as I do tends to shorten the rising periods, but more important is the fact that they improve the appearance, flavor, and texture of any bread.

And to those superior persons who think that anyone who can read a recipe can bake bread, I would say that there are as many poor recipes as there are poor bakers. It takes practice and a knowledge of ingredients and methods to recognize whether a recipe is good and useable. Pity the poor little new cook who decides to try a recipe which sounds good, clipped from the pages of a local paper. Perhaps it was a good recipe the first time it was printed, but it has been reprinted, clipped, filed to be used as a column filler, reprinted and clipped again, several times. Typographical errors have not been corrected, but still it is used. Neither the Woman's Page Editor nor any of her assistants are familiar with breadmaking and notice nothing wrong. Then the poor new baker finds out the hard way that the recipe does not work and she is apt to think it is her fault and is discouraged from trying again.

Let me give you just three examples, taken from the woman's page of a city paper, of recipes that just won't work. The first recipe directed the cook to scald one cup of milk and crumble into it one cake of compressed yeast. Now, the person who did not know that the milk must be cooled to just warm before adding the yeast has ruined her chances of success in the very first step of the mixing procedure. The second recipe directs that the flour should be added in two portions at different times during the mixing, but the list of ingredients gives only the amount of flour for the first portion. Again the result is a complete failure and another would-be breadmaker is discouraged. The third recipe for filled sweet rolls gives directions for forming the dough into round buns, but gives no instructions as to how to fill them. I shudder to think of all the wasted burnt filling to be cleaned from oven floors after the filling had been spread over the rounded tops of the raised buns to melt and run over the edges of the pan during the baking period. Even the most elaborate, deluxe cook books sometimes let a typographical error slip by, usually in the time or temperature of the baking period.

Ann Batchelder, my favorite cooking authority, who for many years endeared herself to the readers of the *Ladies' Home Journal* with her delightful conversational style of writing recipes, wrote in her own cook book that once upon a time every housewife worth her salt baked bread for her family, and that the unforgettable fragrant odor of bread fresh from the oven should be a part of every person's memories. Why should it be just a memory? There are very few housewifes but who could make this tempting, tantalizing odor a present experience. Of course, if too many people were to become proficient in the art of breadmaking, we old-timers would have to divide our compliments with them and reduce equally our sense of self-satisfaction in being one of a small group to keep an almost lost art alive.

I noticed in a recently published article on how to relax, the statement that thinking of the pleasantest taste you can remember, such as a slice of freshly baked, oven-warm bread with butter, would help to relieve tension. If the memory of a slice of bread could do this, think what a great tranquilizer it would be to have a real home-baked loaf available, to actually cut and eat that slice of bread instead of just thinking about it.

I wonder why it is that slices of bread rank higher in memories than rolls or other forms. Could it be that the memory of being allowed to cut a thick slice from a whole loaf makes the remembering that much more pleasant? I know many young people who come to the house are thrilled to see an unsliced loaf and ask to be allowed to do their own cutting. I know that providing guests with uncut loaves and a good sharp knife, causes more reminiscing about the "bread that Mother used to make" than any stack of perfect, thin slices or tray of beautiful rolls of various kinds and shapes. An elderly retired judge recently told me that he would give up all of any elaborate meal for just one slice of homemade bread and butter. Evidently his will power was not strong enough to limit himself to just one for at least three times during the evening he was observed helping himself to a slice of bread.

Mrs. Rorer, a famous early day cooking expert, had some very interesting ideas about baking. She believed that the sun had a good influence on the quality of the bread and urged that all breadmaking be done on bright sunshiny mornings. Be it morning or afternoon, if there is a nice warm spot of sunshine I always set the bowl of dough directly in it and feel very good about it. Many recipes, especially in the older books, directed that the covered bowl be placed in a warm dark cupboard during the rising period.

11

The very idea is distasteful to me. Mrs. Rorer and I are of one mind about the sunshine, but she strongly disapproved of the bread which I enjoy making more than any other. She had made tests proving she thought that Salt Rising Bread could not be processed in a dust-free room, therefore the sponge must contain harmful bacteria that surely could not be good for human consumption. This has not deterred me one bit from enjoying the process of making the ferment for this bread, and more than anything I like the long period of kneading that it requires for the dough to reach that stage of crepe-y resiliency that foretells a perfect loaf with creamy-bisque colored crust and an aroma like nothing else in the world.

Some years ago Dorothy Thompson wrote in the introduction to a well-known book on bread baking, that this would now be an almost breadless nation were it not for the people coming from foreign lands with the taste of homemade bread still with them. Now that the world is so much smaller, and so many of our people are traveling abroad, they are finding out firsthand how these foreign breads taste. They return wanting to learn how to make them in their own homes, to share with friends and to refresh their memories of the places where they had enjoyed eating abroad.

I am including in this little book those recipes, both foreign and domestic, which are the most popular in my small circle of acquaintances in a fairly representative community. Home breadmaking is not a very formal occupation, and I am not a very formal person so this will be a most informal book. Modern commercial breadmaking is a very scientific business, but my knowledge of science is practically nil, so my explanations of my methods will probably be the most unscientific ever offered. I only know that the way I mix my bread doughs gives me better results than when I try other people's methods. I presume other people like the results also because many of them ask for my recipes.

I learned about the use of ginger as a yeast "improver" in one of my very old cook books. The idea appealed to me, I tried it, the results were perfect and I have used it ever since.

From my son's grade school science textbook I learned that salt retards the growth of yeast and should not be added to a yeast mixture until it had grown strong and lively. So I no longer added the salt to a bread sponge until the dissolved yeast had a chance to feed on the sugar and starch, starting a lively crop of new cells. Too much sugar also will somewhat retard the action of the yeast, so it is best to put the major part of the sweetness, when desired, on top, as with sugar-crusted coffee cakes and glazed sweet rolls.

From another cookbook in my collection I learned that grease also retards yeast by coating the cells, thus making them slippery so that they cannot support each other and flatten out. If they are first coated with flour, it helps them to cling together and climb up, round and bubbly, as they grow and divide. This sounded so reasonable to me that I tried mixing a portion of the flour with the yeast mixture before adding the shortening, and the results were amazing. I found that some recipes, such as the one for Saffron Fruit Bread, now gave perfect results without changing a single ingredient, just by using this different method of mixing. I had tried this particular recipe several times and was never happy with it before.

I do not like the term "lukewarm" to describe a temperature. It sounds so inactive and dull. There should be nothing inactive about the process of breadmaking from beginning to end. The meaning of "warm" should vary according to the weather for successful results. On a hot summer day the liquid for the yeast mixture should be barely warm to the touch, and the other ingredients at room temperature. On a cold day the liquid should be comfortably warm to the touch, and the other ingredients may be warmed slightly. Nothing that feels hot to the touch should ever be added to a bread dough. Also the pans in which the bread rises should never feel hot, but just comfortably warm.

To "knead thoroughly" does not mean a few lackadaisical punches and pats. It does mean lifting the dough with fingers spread to support it from underneath, folding over and pushing down hard with the heels of the hands, turning, lifting, folding and pushing down, over and over again until the dough feels RIGHT. With practice one can soon recognize when the kneading has been sufficient.

To "stir until the dough clears the bowl," stir the flour down around the sides of the bowl, instead of into the middle, until they are clean and dry, then the dough turns out easily without scraping even though the ingredients are not yet completely mixed. Spread the flour to be kneaded in around in a ring with only a light coating of flour in the center of the ring, then only as much flour as is needed to make the dough of the proper stiffness may be worked in as the dough is folded and lifted. It is impossible to give the amount of flour exactly, because of the difference in flours, the difference in kneading techniques, and the amount of moisture in the other ingredients aside from the liquid used.

Although we live on a farm, we buy our milk to use for all purposes. Since there is a member of the family on a high-protein low-fat diet I use a great deal of dried skim milk in my cooking and in practically all baking that calls for milk. By using the amount called for to make one quart of reconstituted milk with one pint of liquid, one can double the amount of milk protein without increasing the amount of bread. The bread made with dried skim milk browns more

14

evenly, the crust is more tender, and the crumb does not become hard and dry when cold as with fresh milk breads. However if one wishes to use fresh milk it may be substituted in equal measure for the water or other liquid mixed with the portion of flour to which the yeast mixture is added. It must be first heated to scalding point watching carefully for it scorches very quickly, and then cooled to barely warm or comfortably warm before using. Never use it for the liquid in which to dissolve the yeast.

I prefer to use lard or butter for all recipes except those few which call for a special fat such as oil or bacon fat, but any good vegetable shortening may be used in place of the lard and margarine instead of butter if one wishes.

There are two big important "Don'ts" when it comes to baking bread; No. 1—Don't start a batch of bread unless you are reasonably sure that you are going to have enough time to properly complete the process. No. 2—Don't start a batch of bread until you have read the recipe all the way through, know that you have the proper ingredients or suitable substitutes, and understand the mixing method.

There are also big important "Do's" when it comes to baking bread; No. 1—Do, if you are just learning to bake, try a basic recipe first, such as Perfect White Bread. Observe everything that happens as you proceed through each step. Observe how the yeast mixture looks when it is ready to use, how the dough feels and looks when it has been kneaded sufficiently, how the weight of the loaf feels when it is ready for the oven, what happens to it during the baking period and you will soon know how to make bread you are proud of in every way. No. 2—Do, as soon as you are confident of your breadmaking ability, use your imagination, change the spices, seasonings, flavorings, combinations of fruits and nuts, sizes and shapes of loaves and rolls. Never let your breadmaking become monotonous. Try ingredients which you have never known anyone else to use. Our grand-mothers did this as a matter of necessity. Almost any vegetable which contains a sizeable amount of starch can be used just as potatoes are in bread. Parsnips, turnips, dried peas, lentils, and navy beans may be used after cooking in unsalted water, drained and put through a sieve. I have not yet tried red kidney beans but I intend to. I imagine that they will not make a bread with a very attractive color. Then the problem will be what to add to improve it. I had this problem with the recipes for Peasant's Black Bread and the Flemish Marble Bread. I knew that in early days vegetable juices such as those from carrots and sugar beets were boiled down to a thick, almost black, caramelized syrup to color bread. Parched or scorched grains were used also both to darken the color and to give the bread extra flavor. It was not practical for me to do these things but I did have in my kitchen Postum made from toasted cereals with a very dark color when dissolved in a small amount of water. I also had Kitchen Bouquet which is made from the juices of vegetables and caramelized sugar. So, I had found just the right two ingredients to improve color and flavor already prepared for me. Tomorrow I may think of something else in a bottle or jar on the shelf that I just can't wait to see how it works when added to a certain recipe.

My gas oven is new and the temperature range has been thoroughly checked for accuracy, therefore I am giving the temperature settings which give best results for me. If your oven has not been checked recently, or if it is other than a gas oven, check your baking at frequent intervals the first time a certain recipe is used. If you should need to set your oven at a different temperature for best results, make a note of it near the recipe. Then the next time you will know where to set the temperature control and will not have to watch your baking so closely.

No matter how much one enjoys baking with yeast, quick breads made with baking powder and soda have an important place in the baking schedule for any family, so I am including a few of those that my family like best. I will have to admit, though, that I never have the feeling of full accomplishment when a pan of quick bread comes from the oven as I do with a loaf or a pan of "just-right" rolls made with yeast. The greatest sense of complete satisfaction comes from producing a perfectly beautiful loaf of bread by using a bread starter and "projecting" it from the beginning as our pioneer women had to do, using no commercial yeast at all.

I sincerely hope that the users of this book will get at least a fraction of the pleasure from it that I enjoyed from the task of selecting, retesting (which included tasting too often and too much), checking and putting together this collection. There is no luck involved where breadmaking is concerned. It is all a matter of practice, understanding methods, and observation of every step of the process until you are thoroughly familiar with it. And so I do not wish you luck, but success with every recipe you try.

Ada Lou Roberts

Editorial note: One cake of compressed yeast and one package of dry yeast may be used interchangeably.

I AM MANY WOMEN

When sky and street merge in sullen grayness
and black trees stir in sleep,
my stove becomes a hearth.
I am many women who have looked at rain
through a flap of hide, from a hand hewn door,
and felt secure against a threatening world,
blessed within warm walls and sheltering roof.
Hands deep in flour,
powdered grain from a million fields
garnered in sweating sunlight,
I am many women who have kneaded resilient dough
with strong hands . . .
brown, red, yellow and white hands.
Folding and stretching, shaping
smoothly contoured loaves
rich with the smell of yeast.
(Bread is like nothing so much as bread,
sacred in its own identity.)
The sky trades snow for night,
and the scent of baking loaves
is calm benediction for my home.
I am many women who have taken bread from an oven,
and breaking it . . .
felt consecrated.

Courtesy PATTI LINN *and* GOURMET MAGAZINE

PERFECT WHITE BREAD

½ cup warm water	4 cups flour
1 teaspoon sugar	¾ cup dried skim milk
¼ teaspoon ginger	3 cups warm water
2 packages dry yeast	5 teaspoons salt
⅓ cup sugar	½ cup soft lard
2½ cups warm water	10 cups flour

Combine the first 4 ingredients and let stand in a warm place until bubbling nicely. In a large bowl stir together ⅓ cup sugar, 2½ cups water, 4 cups flour and ¾ cup dried skim milk. Stir in the yeast mixture, beating well. Cover the bowl and let stand in a warm place until the sponge is well risen and bubbly. Add 3 cups warm water, 5 teaspoons salt, and ½ cup lard and beat well. Stir in 8 cups flour, mixing until the dough clears the bowl. Spread the remaining 2 cups of flour on the pastry board, turn out the dough and knead well, using a little additional flour if necessary to make it smooth and satiny. Return to the bowl, dust top of dough with flour, cover with a damp cloth, and let rise in a warm place for about 30 minutes. Turn out, knead thoroughly, using only enough flour to keep dough from sticking. Divide into even portions, shape into loaves, place in greased pans, brush tops of loaves with soft lard, and allow to rise again until double in bulk. Bake in preheated oven for 45 minutes; the first 20 minutes at 350° F., then reduce heat to 325° F. for the rest of the baking period. If a very soft crust is desired, brush tops of loaves with melted lard or butter as soon as they are removed from the oven and allow to stand for about 5 minutes before removing from the pans. This recipe makes 6 medium sized loaves.

SHREDDED WHEAT PECAN BREAD

1 cup hot water	¾ cup dried skim milk
3 shredded whole-wheat biscuits	½ cup Brer Rabbit Molasses
½ cup warm water	4 tablespoons soft lard
1 teaspoon sugar	2 teaspoons salt
¼ teaspoon ginger	1½ cups pecans, coarsely broken
2 packages dry yeast	8 cups flour
2½ cups warm water	
4 cups flour	

Pour the 1 cup of hot water over the shredded biscuits and let stand to soak. Combine the next 4 ingredients and let stand in a warm place until bubbling nicely. In a large bowl stir together 2½ cups warm water, 4 cups flour and ¾ cup dried skim milk. Add the yeast mixture and beat well. Add the molasses, lard, salt, 6 cups of flour and pecan meats, stirring the pecans into the flour to coat them before mixing into the dough. Add the biscuits and water in which they were soaking. Stir all together until the dough clears the bowl. Spread the remaining 2 cups of flour on the pastry board, turn out the dough and knead well, using a little more flour if necessary. This must be a fairly stiff dough. Return to bowl, grease top of dough, cover and let rise until double in bulk. Turn out, work down and divide into portions for loaves of any size desired. I like to bake this in round loaves in heavy aluminum pudding pans which are 8 inches in diameter and 3 inches deep. This recipe will make three such loaves. Grease the pans well and dust with flour. Form dough into balls, roll in flour, coating with as much as will stick to the dough, place in the centers of the pans, flatten balls a little and sprinkle a little more flour on tops. Cover and let rise until double in bulk. Bake in oven preheated to 350° F. for 45 minutes. For marvelous Melba toast, slice as thinly as possible across loaf and dry the whole big slices in a very low oven until crisp, brittle and just tinged with brown. These are wonderful to serve with almost anything; salads, soups, bowls of fresh sugared fruit, or coffee.

COUNTRY BRAIDS

½ cup warm water	1 cup warm water
1 teaspoon sugar	½ cup sugar
¼ teaspoon ginger	¼ soft butter
2 packages dry yeast	1 teaspoon salt
2 cups flour	2 eggs, well beaten
½ cup dried skim milk	3 cups flour

Combine the first 4 ingredients and let stand in a warm place until bubbling nicely. In a large mixing bowl mix together 2 cups of flour, ½ cup of dried skim milk, 1 cup of warm water and ½ cup of sugar. Add the yeast mixture and beat well. Add ¼ cup of soft butter, 1 teaspoon of salt, 2 eggs and 2 cups of flour. Stir all together until the dough clears the bowl. Spread the remaining 1 cup of flour on the pastry board, turn out the dough and knead thoroughly, using a little more flour if necessary, to make a smooth, elastic dough. Return to the bowl, brush top of dough with butter, cover with towel and let stand until double in bulk, about 1 to 1¼ hours. Turn out the dough, knead well, divide into halves, and then divide each half into 3 equal portions. Roll each portion into a strip about 8 to 10 inches long. Cross 3 rolls in the center and braid to each end. Pinch ends tightly together and place braid on a greased cookie sheet. Braid remaining rolls and place on top of first braid. Cover with a barely damp towel or a sheet of Saran Wrap and let rise until double in bulk. Brush with beaten egg yolk thinned with 1 teaspoon of water, and sprinkle with salt or sugar, whichever you prefer. Bake in oven preheated to 375° F. for about 30 minutes. The crust will have a golden glaze.

MOLASSES WHOLE WHEAT BREAD

½ cup warm water	½ cup dried skim milk
1 teaspoon sugar	¾ cup warm water
¼ teaspoon ginger	1½ teaspoons salt
2 packages dry yeast	3 tablespoons melted
1 cup warm water	butter
5 tablespoons molasses	4 cups whole-wheat flour
2 cups whole-wheat flour	

Combine the first 4 ingredients and let stand in a warm place until bubbling nicely. In a large bowl stir together 1 cup warm water, molasses, 2 cups whole-wheat flour and the dried skim milk. Beat in the yeast mixture, cover the bowl and let rise in a warm place until the sponge is light and foamy. Add ¾ cup warm water, salt, butter and 3 cups whole-wheat flour. Stir until the dough clears the bowl. Spread the remaining 1 cup of flour on the pastry board, turn out the dough and knead until smooth and stiff, using a little more flour if necessary. (This bread has a coarse texture and will not hold up unless the dough is stiff.) Return to the bowl, grease top of dough lightly, cover and allow to rise until double in bulk. Turn, out, knead well, divide into halves, shape into loaves, place in greased pans, brush tops with melted butter and let rise until the pans feel light when lifted. Bake in oven preheated to 350° F. for about 45 minutes. (Honey or sorghum may be used with equally good results in place of the molasses. But never, never combine honey and sorghum unless you have an effective air-freshener handy, for the smell is most unpleasant during the baking process and lingers in the bread itself.) This is a delicious bread to bake on a day when Apple Butter is also being made, for they make a wonderful combination which can be even more satisfactory when a glass of briskly cold buttermilk is at hand also.

WHEAT GERM BREAD

½ cup warm water	2 cups flour
1 teaspoon sugar	¾ cup dried skim milk
¼ teaspoon ginger	3 tablespoons soft lard
2 packages dry yeast	1½ teaspoons salt
1½ cups warm water	2 cups wheat germ
2 tablespoons honey	4 cups flour

Combine the first 4 ingredients and let set in a warm place until bubbling nicely. In a large bowl stir together 1½ cups warm water, 2 tablespoons honey, 2 cups flour and ¾ cup dried skim milk. Add the yeast mixture and beat well. Add 3 tablespoons lard, 1½ teaspoons salt, 2 cups wheat germ and 3 cups flour. Stir until the dough clears the bowl. Spread the remaining 1 cup of flour on the pastry board, turn out the dough and knead thoroughly, using a little more flour if necessary to make a smooth dough. Return to bowl, grease top of dough, cover and allow to stand in warm place until double in bulk. Turn out dough, knead lightly, divide into halves and shape into 2 large loaves. Place in well greased pans, brush tops of loaves with butter, and let rise again until light. Bake in oven preheated to 350° F. for about 40 minutes. Again brush tops of loaves with butter, turn pans on sides and allow loaves to cool for a few minutes before removing from the pans. (By omitting salt from the recipe, this makes a very good bread for a low-salt or salt-free diet. The combination of honey and wheat germ gives such a nut-like, wholesome flavor that the absence of salt is not noticeable).

REMEMBER—*Breads made with molasses or honey brown more quickly than others. Bake as near the center of the oven as possible.*

CANADIAN RUSKS

½ cup warm water	6 eggs, well beaten
1 teaspoon sugar	1 teaspoon salt
¼ teaspoon ginger	4 tablespoons soft butter
2 packages dry yeast	8 cups flour
1 cup warm water	
6 tablespoons sugar	sugar
2 cups flour	cinnamon
¾ cup dried skim milk	Instant Coffee

Combine the first 4 ingredients and let stand in a warm place until bubbling nicely. In a large bowl mix together 1 cup warm water, 6 tablespoons sugar, 2 cups flour and ¾ cups dried skim milk. Beat well and add the yeast mixture. Cover and let stand in a warm place until light and spongy. Add the 6 eggs, well beaten, 1 teaspoon salt, 4 tablespoons soft butter and 6 cups of flour. Stir until the dough clears the bowl. Spread the remaining 2 cups flour on the pastry board, turn out dough and knead thoroughly. Use a little more flour if necessary to make a smooth, elastic, but quite stiff dough. Return to bowl, grease top of dough, cover and let rise until double in bulk. Turn out, knead well and divide into 4 portions. Form each portion into a flattened roll 12 to 14 inches in length and about 4 inches wide. Sprinkle 2 heaping teaspoons of white sugar and 1 teaspoon of cinnamon on a sheet of waxed paper. Turn the roll over and over until the whole surface is coated with the sugar mixture. Use the above amount to coat each roll or substitute 1 teaspoon of Instant Coffee for the cinnamon for some of the rolls. Transfer the rolls to 15-inch-long greased cookie sheets, 2 rolls to a sheet, keeping them as even and straight as possible. Let rise until light, then bake in a slow oven, preheated to 325° F. for 40 minutes. As soon as they are completely cooled, cut each roll crosswise into about ⅓ inch slices. Spread on cookie sheets, cut sides up, and return to oven which is set at as low a temperature as possible. Let dry, turning often, until no moisture remains and the slices are bisque colored. This will take several hours. Store in plastic bags in the freezer, and they can be re-crisped in a matter of minutes. (A note in the old Canadian cook book from which this recipe was adapted states that "the rusks when first baked, eat deliciously, being buttered for tea, and even better when cold." This statement is very true in spite of its odd wording and especially true if you just happen to have a fresh supply of Ozark Jam or other favorite spread to add to the butter. Then I know some people who consider these rusks superior to doughnuts for dunking and casually empty a bag of 12 or 15 slices at one sitting.)

APPLE LAYER COFFEE CAKE

The Canadian Rusk dough may be used to make this coffee cake. Roll ½ the dough into a large rectangle, very thin and about 30 by 15 inches. Place across a jelly roll pan, 15 by 10 by 1 inch, with the center portion of the dough resting in the pan. Spread the center portion of dough with butter, then with ½ of the Apple Filling. Lap one side portion of dough over the center, stretching and fitting it evenly. Spread with butter and the remainder of the filling. Fold over the second side portion of the dough and pinch edges together all the way around the sides and ends. Cut several slits with a sharp knife down through the dough, being careful not to cut through the bottom layer. Brush top with milk, sprinkle with cinnamon and sugar. Let rise until light and puffy. Bake in oven preheated to 325° F. for 45 minutes.

APPLE FILLING

2 cups very thick
  applesauce
½ to 1 cup brown sugar
  (depending on sweet-
  ness of applesauce)

1 cup flaked cocoanut
1 cup Grape-Nuts
1 teaspoon mace
  chopped nuts, if desired

Combine ingredients and mix well. Let stand while dough is being made up so that the Grape-Nuts will soften and thicken the filling to the proper consistency for spreading.

PEPPERED CHEESE BREAD

½ cup warm water
1 teaspoon sugar
¼ teaspoon ginger
2 packages dry yeast
3 cups warm water
4 tablespoons sugar
3 cups flour
¾ cup dried skim milk

4 tablespoons soft
  shortening
2 teaspoons salt
3 eggs, well beaten
2 teaspoons Black Java
  Pepper, coarsely ground
6 cups flour
2 cups dry sharp Cheddar
  cheese, coarsely grated

Combine the first 4 ingredients and let stand in a warm place until bubbling nicely. In a large bowl stir together 3 cups warm water, 4 tablespoons sugar, 3 cups flour, and ¾ cups dried skim milk. Beat in the yeast mixture. Add the 4 table-spoons soft shortening, 2 teaspoons salt, 3 eggs, 2 teaspoons pepper and 5 cups of flour. Stir until the dough clears the bowl. Spread the remaining 1 cup of flour on the pastry board, turn out the dough, and knead well, using a little more flour if necessary. Now, flatten dough with the hands, sprinkle ½ cup of grated cheese over the surface. Roll up dough and flatten again. Repeat the process until all the cheese is worked into the dough. Knead lightly to be sure the cheese is evenly distributed through the dough. Return to the bowl, grease top of dough, cover and allow to rise until light. Turn out, knead down, divide into 6 equal portions, rolling these into even length strips, tapered at each end. Lay 3 strips on each of 2 cookie sheets. Start in the middle and braid strips to each end, pressing the ends down lightly to the pan. Cover with a light, barely damp towel, and allow to rise again until light. Brush tops of braids with an egg yolk, beaten with 2 tablespoons of water. Bake in oven preheated to 350° F. for 20 minutes, then reduce heat to 325 ° F. and continue baking for 25 minutes. Brush again with the egg mixture about 5 minutes before the end of the baking period. (If ever there was a perfect bread to serve fresh and thinly sliced with crisp salads of all kinds, this is it.)

HERB BREAD

½ cup warm water	3 teaspoons Chicken Stock
1 teaspoon sugar	Powder (Spice Island)
¼ teaspoon ginger	½ cup warm water
2 packages dry yeast	1 teaspoon thyme
2 cups warm water	1 teaspoon summer savory
2 tablespoons sugar	1 teaspoon rosemary
3 cups flour	½ cup soft shortening
	5 cups flour

Combine the first 4 ingredients and let stand in a warm place until bubbling nicely. In a large bowl stir together 2 cups warm water, 2 tablespoons sugar, 3 cups flour and 3 teaspoons Chicken Stock Powder dissolved in ½ cup warm water. Add the yeast mixture and beat well. Add the herbs, ½ cup soft shortening, and 4 cups flour. Stir the dough until it clears the bowl. Spread the remaining 1 cup of flour on the pastry board. Turn out the dough and knead thoroughly, using a little more flour if necessary to make a smooth, elastic dough. Return to the bowl, grease top of dough, cover with a towel and let rise until double in bulk. Turn out, knead dough lightly, divide and shape into loaves or rolls as desired. Place in well-greased pans, brush tops with butter, and allow to rise again until double in bulk. Bake in oven preheated to 350° F. for about 45 minutes for loaves, and 20 to 25 minutes for rolls depending on their size. For a glazed crust, place a pan of boiling water on the floor of the oven, and brush top of bread with a beaten egg yolk thinned with 1 teaspoon of water about 5 minutes before the end of the baking period. This recipe makes 2 large loaves. (This bread is very nice to make up into rolls shaped like miniature French loaves about 5 inches long. These are delicious when broken open with a fork when still quite warm and covered with spoonfuls of rich, smooth creamed chicken.)

BROWN RICE BREAD

½ cup warm water	¾ cup dried skim milk
1 teaspoon sugar	6 tablespoons soft butter
¼ teaspoon ginger	3 teaspoons salt
2 packages dry yeast	4 cups cooked, drained,
1½ cups warm water	warm rice
6 tablespoons sugar	6 cups flour
4 cups flour	

Combine the first 4 ingredients and let stand in a warm place until bubbling nicely. In a large bowl stir together 1½ cups warm water, 6 tablespoons sugar, 4 cups flour and ¾ cup dried skim milk. Add the yeast mixture and beat well. Add 6 tablespoons soft butter, 3 teaspoons salt, 4 cups rice and 4 cups flour. Stir until the dough clears the bowl. Spread the remaining 2 cups of flour on the pastry board, turn out the dough, and knead well using a little more flour if necessary to make a stiff dough. (More moisture will be released from the cooked rice during the process of baking, so more flour is needed than for a straight dough.) Return dough to bowl, brush top with butter, cover with a towel and let rise until double in bulk. Turn out, knead thoroughly, divide into even portions, shape into loaves, place in greased pans and allow to rise again until light. Bake in oven preheated to 350° F. for about 45 minutes. Brush tops of loaves with melted butter, turn pans on sides and allow loaves to cool for a few minutes before removing. This recipe makes 4 large loaves.

(To prepare rice: take 1 cup natural long grain brown rice and stir it into 10 cups of rapidly boiling water. It is necessary to use a large amount of water when cooking brown rice to make the grains light and fluffy. Cover tightly, turn heat down low and simmer for 40 minutes. Drain in colander and rinse with cold water until the grains are fluffy and well separated.)

GRAPE-NUTS HONEY BREAD

2 cups Grape-Nuts	2 cups flour
4 tablespoons honey	¾ cup dried skim milk
2 cups warm water	4 tablespoons soft
½ cup warm water	shortening
1 teaspoon sugar	2 teaspoons salt
¼ teaspoon ginger	4 cups flour
2 packages dry yeast	

In a large bowl combine the 2 cups Grape-Nuts, 4 table-spoons honey and 2 cups warm water. Let stand for about 30 minutes until the cereal is soaked and soft. Combine ½ cup warm water, 1 teaspoon sugar, ¼ teaspoon ginger and 2 packages dry yeast. Let stand in a warm place until bubbling nicely. Combine the two mixtures and beat thoroughly. Stir in 2 cups flour and ¾ cup dried skim milk. Add 4 tablespoons soft shortening, 2 teaspoons salt and 3 cups flour. Stir until the dough clears the bowl. Spread the remaining 1 cup flour on the pastry board, turn out the dough and knead well, using a little more flour if necessary to make an elastic, non-sticky dough. Return to the bowl, grease top of dough, cover with towel and let stand until double in bulk. Turn out, knead dough lightly, and shape into loaves. This recipe will make 3 medium-sized loaves. Place in greased pans, brush tops of loaves with butter, and let rise until double in bulk. Bake in oven preheated to 350° F. for 45 minutes. Brush tops of loaves with butter again as soon as they are taken from the oven, and allow to cool for a few minutes before removing from the pans.

(This is a really high-protein bread that, when thinly sliced, makes the crispest of Melba toast. By omitting the 2 tea-spoons of salt from the recipe this makes a very good bread for a low-salt diet; since it has such a pleasant flavor the absence of salt is not noticeable.)

FRENCH BREAD

½ cup warm water
1 teaspoon sugar
¼ teaspoon ginger
1 package dry yeast
4 cups flour
½ cup warm water
1 tablespoon sugar

1 teaspoon salt
2 tablespoons soft
  shortening
2 egg whites, stiffly beaten
1½ teaspoons cornstarch
½ teaspoon salt
½ cup water

Combine the first 4 ingredients and set in a warm place to rise until bubbling nicely. Measure 3½ cups flour into mixing bowl. With a large mixing spoon make a depression in the center of the flour. Into this pour ½ cup warm water, add the 1 tablespoon sugar and the yeast mixture. Stir in a little of the flour to make the yeast mixture slightly thickened. Cover bowl and let stand until the sponge has risen until rounded in the center. Add the salt and shortening, then mix altogether until well blended. Fold in the stiffly beaten egg whites. Spread the remaining ½ cup flour on the pastry board, turn out dough and knead thoroughly, using a little more flour if necessary to make a smooth stiff dough. Return to bowl, cover with a damp towel and let rise until doubled in bulk. Turn out, knead dough lightly and divide in half. Shape into two long loaves tapered at the ends. Place on baking sheet sprinkled with corn meal. Cover with damp towel, or slip into a large plastic bag and let rise again until light, but not so long that the bubbles begin to burst on the surface. While the loaves are rising, cook the cornstarch, salt and ½ cup water until thick and clear, then let cool. Brush the surface of the loaves thickly with this glaze. Cut diagonal slashes the length of the loaves about ½ inch deep. Bake in oven pre-heated to 400 degrees and with pan of water on floor of oven, for 15 minutes, reduce heat to 350 degrees and bake 25 to 30 minutes longer until bread sounds hollow when tapped. Cool on rack. Do not wrap this bread tightly, if you wish the crust to stay crisp and hard.

FLEMISH MARBLE BREAD

½ cup warm water
1 teaspoon sugar
¼ teaspoon ginger
2 packages dry yeast
2½ cups warm water
¾ cup light sorghum
3 cups white flour

¾ cup dried skim milk
4 tablespoons soft butter
3 teaspoons salt
3½ cups white flour
1 teaspoon Kitchen
Bouquet
3 cups whole-wheat flour
½ cup white flour

Combine the first 4 ingredients and let stand in a warm place until bubbling nicely. In a large bowl stir together 2½ cups water, ¾ cup light sorghum, 3 cups white flour and ¾ cup dried skim milk. Add the yeast mixture and beat well. Cover bowl and let stand in a warm place until a light sponge forms. Add 4 tablespoons butter and 3 teaspoons salt; beat well. Divide this sponge in halves. To the first half add 3 cups white flour and stir until the dough clears the bowl. Spread the remaining ½ cup flour on the pastry board, turn out dough and knead well. Grease ball of dough all over and return to bowl. To the second half of the sponge add 1 teaspoon Kitchen Bouquet and 3 cups whole-wheat flour. Stir until the dough clears the bowl. Spread the ½ cup white flour on the pastry board, turn out dough and knead well. Grease ball of dough and place in bowl beside white portion. Cover and let rise until light. Turn out balls of dough separately, knead lightly, and for 3 medium-sized loaves divide each ball of dough into 6 equal portions. Shape each portion into a roll slightly longer than the loaf pan to be used. For each loaf twist 2 rolls of white and 2 rolls of brown dough together tightly but without intermixing the doughs. Pinch tightly together at the ends and place in the greased pans. Brush tops of loaves with butter, cover lightly with towel, and let rise until light. Allow plenty of time for the brown dough will be

a little slower in raising than the white. Bake in oven preheated to 350° F. for about 50 minutes. About 5 minutes before end of baking period brush tops of loaves with milk.
(This recipe is perfect for making a variety of rolls, such as
the following:

HALF 'N' HALF MUFFIN ROLLS

Place two small balls, one each of white and brown, in each
well-greased muffin ring. Make the white ball slightly smaller
than the brown, to have the two of equal size when baked.
Brush tops with butter, cover with towel, let rise until very
light, brush tops with milk and bake for about 25 minutes in
350° F. oven.

LUCKY CLOVER ROLLS

Place four tiny balls, two each of white and brown dough in
each muffin ring and proceed according to directions given
above.

FAN TANS

Roll out equal portions of white and brown dough into oblongs about ¼ inch thick. Spread butter thickly on white
oblong, place brown dough layer on top and spread it
thickly with butter. Cut into three strips about 1½ inches
wide. Stack one on top of other, making six layers of dough.
Slice into sections about 1 inch thick and place in greased
muffin rings, cut side down. Proceed with rising and baking
period according to directions given above.

REMEMBER—*Never let your bakings become monotonous. Try
a new recipe. Make different sized and shaped loaves and
rolls.*

DOUBLE KNOT ROLLS

Shape an equal number of finger sized rolls about 5 inches long, from the white and brown dough. Lay one roll of each together, holding the two rolls together at one end, make loop and pull the other two ends through to make a loose knot. Lay on greased cookie sheet, far enough apart so as not to touch when raised. Proceed with rising and baking period according to directions given above.

ITALIAN BREAD

½ cup warm water	2 cups warm water
1 teaspoon sugar	2 tablespoons sugar
¼ teaspoon ginger	1½ teaspoons salt
2 packages dry yeast	2 tablespoons olive or
5 cups flour	vegetable oil
	1 cup flour

Combine the first 4 ingredients and let stand in a warm place until bubbling nicely. Measure the 5 cups of flour into a deep mixing bowl. With large spoon form a deep depression in the flour by pressing it out from the center and up on the sides of the bowl. Pour the 2 cups of water into this depression, add the 2 tablespoons sugar and the yeast mixture. With spoon gently work in enough flour from the rim to slightly thicken the liquid mixture. Cover bowl and let stand until the sponge is foamy and beginning to round up in the center. Add the salt and oil. Now stir in the rest of the flour from the sides of the bowl. This will be almost too stiff to stir until well mixed. Spread the remaining 1 cup of flour on the pastry board, turn out dough and knead for 10 minutes or more, working in all the flour possible. Work until the ball of dough is smooth and heavy as a ball of putty, and does not stick even to an unfloured portion of the board. Return to bowl, brush top of dough with oil, cover and let rise until doubled in bulk. Turn out dough, knead lightly, and shape into long tapered loaves. This recipe will make 2 loaves about

15 inches long and about 5 inches wide that can be baked on 1 large cookie sheet lengthwise, or 2 shorter, thicker loaves to bake crosswise of the sheet. Sprinkle the cookie sheet thickly with white corn meal. Place the loaves on sheet so that they will not touch when raised. Make diagonal slashes with knife across tops, about 2 in. apart. Slip into a large plastic bag and let rise until almost doubled in bulk. (If the dough becomes too light the bubbles will begin to break on surface and the crust will not be strong enough to hold the loaf from flattening out as it bakes.) Brush with a beaten egg white diluted with 2 tablespoons water. Bake on center rack of oven preheated to 350° F. for 45 minutes. Place a pan of steaming hot water on floor of oven during baking period for a perfect shell crust. The dough in the center of loaves will bulge up and burst through the crust at intervals, which gives the tops their interesting contrast of smooth and rough surfaces.

ITALIAN SEEDED BREAD

Immediately after brushing the tops of the loaves with the egg white glaze sprinkle thickly with poppy, celery, sesame, or caraway seed. It is very nice to make little individual loaves from this dough, about 4 inches long and 2 inches wide, and seed the crusts with all 4 varieties of seeds so that guests may take their choice.

TIGER CRUST BREAD

About 10 minutes before loaves are ready for the oven, put ½ teaspoon yeast and 1 teaspoon sugar to soak in 2 tablespoons warm water. When it bubbles, stir in 2 tablespoons arrowroot or cornstarch and 1 teaspoon oil. Let stand until just before placing loaves in the oven. Stir down bubbles, and brush thickly over surface of loaves. This glaze will crackle as it bakes forming an interesting mottled "tiger" pattern on the crust.

FIG AND NUT YEAST BREAD

½ cup warm water	4 tablespoons soft butter
1 teaspoon sugar	1½ teaspoons salt
¼ teaspoon ginger	1½ cups soft dried figs,
2 packages dry yeast	chopped fine
1½ cups warm water	1½ cups black or English
4 tablespoons Brer	walnuts, chopped
Rabbit molasses	1 cup white flour
2 cups whole-wheat flour	4 cups whole-wheat flour
½ cup dried skim milk	

Combine the first 4 ingredients and let stand in a warm place until bubbling nicely. In a large bowl stir together 1½ cups warm water, 2 cups whole-wheat flour and ½ cup dried skim milk. Add the yeast mixture and beat well. Add the 4 table-spoons butter, 1½ teaspoons salt, the figs and the nut meats well dusted with 1 cup white flour, and 3 cups whole-wheat flour. Stir until the dough clears the bowl. Spread the re-maining 1 cup whole-wheat flour on the pastry board, turn out dough and knead thoroughly, using a little more white flour if necessary to make a fairly stiff, non-sticky dough. Return to the bowl, brush top of dough with butter, cover and let rise until double in bulk. Turn out, knead lightly and divide into portions. Shape into loaves, either long or round, place in well-greased pans, brush tops with butter and allow to rise again until light. Bake in oven preheated to 350° F. for about 60 minutes. Watch carefully, as any dough con-taining molasses browns more quickly than a straight dough. Do not place loaves too near the walls of the oven, and either bake them on a center shelf of the oven or change them from the lower to upper shelf about the middle of the baking period. This recipe makes 5 small loaves.

DUTCH PRUNE BREAD

½ cup warm water	1½ teaspoons salt
1 teaspoon sugar	3 eggs, well beaten
¼ teaspoon ginger	½ cup soft butter
2 packages dry yeast	1 teaspoon cinnamon
1½ cups warm water	2 tablespoons lemon rind
½ cup sugar	2 cups cooked, drained,
2 cups flour	chopped prunes
½ cup dried skim milk	6 cups flour

Combine the first 4 ingredients and let stand in a warm place until bubbling nicely. In a large bowl stir together 1½ cups warm water, ½ cup sugar, 2 cups flour and ½ cup dried skim milk. Add the yeast mixture and beat well. Add 1½ teaspoons salt, 3 eggs, well beaten, ½ cup soft butter, 1 teaspoon cinnamon, 2 tablespoons lemon rind, 2 cups prunes and 5 cups flour. Stir until the dough clears the bowl. Spread the remaining 1 cup of flour on the pastry board, turn out the dough and knead thoroughly, using a little more flour if necessary. Return to the bowl, brush top of dough with butter, cover and let rise until double in bulk. Turn out dough, knead lightly, divide into equal portions, shape into loaves, and place in greased pans. Brush tops with butter and allow to rise until double in bulk. Bake in oven preheated to 350° F. for 45 to 50 minutes for medium-sized loaves. This recipe makes 3 medium-sized loaves. I like to bake a part of the dough in No. 2½ size tin fruit cans. Make the dough into balls that will about half fill the cans, and let rise to within about an inch of the top cans before placing in the oven. Bake for about 30 minutes. (These tall round loaves make very attractive slices for sandwiches or for toasting.)

REMEMBER—*Doughs containing heavy ingredients such as nut, candied fruits, raisins, etc. require a longer period of time for raising than straight doughs.*

PRUNE AND CARROT BREAD

½ cup warm water
1 teaspoon sugar
¼ teaspoon ginger
2 packages dry yeast
1 cup warm water
½ cup honey
2 cups flour
½ cup dried skim milk

2 cups cooked, chopped prunes
2 cups grated, raw carrots
2 teaspoons salt
4 tablespoons soft shortening (butter preferred)
6 cups flour

Combine the first 4 ingredients and let stand in a warm place until bubbling nicely. In a large bowl stir together 1 cup warm water, ½ cup honey, 2 cups flour and ½ cup dried skim milk. Add the yeast mixture and beat well. Add the 2 cups prunes, 2 cups carrots, 2 teaspoons salt, 4 tablespoons shortening and 4 cups flour. Stir until the dough clears the bowl. Spread the remaining 2 cups flour on the pastry board, turn out the dough and knead thoroughly, using a little more flour if necessary until a very elastic, non-sticky dough is formed. (The prunes and carrots will release additional moisture during the baking process so the dough must be quite stiff.) Return to the bowl, brush top of dough with butter, cover and allow to rise until double in bulk. Turn out dough, knead lightly, divide into portions and shape into loaves. This recipe will make 4 medium-sized loaves. Place in well-greased pans, brush tops of loaves with butter and let stand until light. Place in oven preheated to 350° F. for 25 minutes, then if it appears that the crust will become too brown, reduce heat to 325° F. for the last 20 minutes. For an extra soft rich crust brush tops of loaves generously with butter about 5 minutes before the end of the baking period. (This dough will require about twice as long a time for rising as a straight dough, but the results are well worth waiting for. It is delicious to serve with just butter as soon as cool enough to slice.)

APPLE RAISIN BREAD

½ cup warm water	2 cups (1 pound can)
1 teaspoon sugar	unsweetened applesauce
¼ teaspoon ginger	4 tablespoons soft
2 packages dry yeast	shortening
1 cup warm water	2 teaspoons salt
½ cup sugar	5 (or more) cups flour
2 cups flour	2 cups seeded raisins
¾ cup dried skim milk	

Combine the first 4 ingredients and let stand in a warm place until bubbling nicely. In a large bowl stir together 1 cup water, ½ cup sugar, 2 cups flour and ¾ cup dried skim milk. Add the yeast mixture and beat well. Add the 2 cups applesauce (at room temperature or slightly warmer), 4 tablespoons shortening, 2 teaspoons salt and 4 cups flour. Stir until the dough clears the bowl. Spread 1 cup of flour on the pastry board, turn out dough and knead until smooth, using more flour if necessary (some applesauce contains more moisture than others so the exact amount of flour cannot be given). Knead in the raisins, a handful at a time, as the last of the flour is being worked in. Continue to knead until the raisins are well distributed. Return dough to bowl, brush top with shortening, cover with towel and let rise until double in bulk. Turn out, knead lightly, divide into portions, form into desired shapes, place in greased pans, cover lightly and let rise again until light. Bake in oven preheated to 350° F. about 50 minutes for large loaves, 40 minutes for medium loaves and about 25 minutes for a Coffee round. Makes 2 large loaves.

MARSHMALLOW COFFEE ROUND

Roll a portion of the dough given above into a circle about ½-inch thick to fit a round cake pan. Brush top of dough with thick cream or evaporated milk, sprinkle lightly with sugar and cinnamon. Let rise until very light. Bake about 25 minutes, remove from oven, space enough marshmallows over the top so that they will touch when melted. Sprinkle a few chopped nuts or chocolate bits between the marshmallows, place under the broiler until melted enough to spread and delicately toasted. Serve while warm. Cut with a knife blade dipped in boiling water and the topping will not drag and wrinkle.

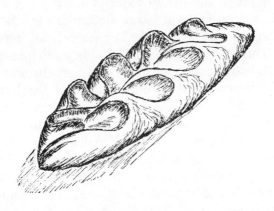

SAVORY BARLEY BREAD

1 cup pearl barley	2 cups warm water
3 cups water	4 tablespoons sugar
½ cup warm water	2 cups flour
1 teaspoon sugar	½ cup soft butter
¼ teaspoon ginger	2 teaspoons seasoning salt
2 packages dry yeast	6 cups flour

Simmer 1 cup barley in 3 cups water for 30 to 40 minutes until it absorbs all the water and is tender. Let cool until just barely warm before adding to the bread dough. Combine the next 4 ingredients and let stand in warm place until bubbling nicely. In a large bowl stir together 2 cups warm water, 4 tablespoons sugar and 2 cups flour. Add the yeast mixture and beat well. Add ½ cup butter and 2 teaspoons seasoning salt (plain salt may be used if the spicy herb taste is not desired). Add 4 cups flour and the slightly warm, cooked barley. Stir until the dough clears the bowl. Spread the remaining 2 cups of flour on the pastry board, turn out the dough and knead vigorously, using more flour if necessary as the heaviness of the barley requires a fairly stiff dough to hold it in suspension as it bakes. Return to the bowl, grease top of dough, cover and let rise in a warm place until double in bulk. Turn out, knead lightly, divide into equal portions, shape into loaves and place in greased pans. Brush tops with melted butter and let stand until light. This dough rises very quickly, if kept at the proper temperature, so do not let it become over-light. Bake in oven preheated to 350° F. for about 45 minutes for medium-sized loaves. Brush tops of loaves with butter again about 5 minutes before the end of the baking period. Turn pans on sides and allow to cool for a few minutes before removing from pans. This recipe makes 5 medium-sized loaves. This fragrant bread goes perfectly with a plain lettuce or mixed vegetable salad, and a variety of cheese. There is nothing better to use in making toasted tomato and bacon, or roast beef sandwiches.)

PEAR BREAD

½ cup warm water	½ cup soft butter
1 teaspoon sugar	2 teaspoons salt
¼ teaspoon ginger	4 eggs, well beaten
2 packages dry yeast	2 cups dried pears,
1 cup warm pear juice	softened and chopped
½ cup honey	1 to 2 teaspoons almond
2 cups flour	flavoring
½ cup dried skim milk	5 cups flour

(Put 1 pound dried pears to soak in hot water just to cover. Let stand overnight. In the morning remove any hard core sections, chop and measure 2 cups of drained pears.) Combine the first 4 ingredients and let stand in a warm place until bubbling nicely. In a large bowl stir together 1 cup warm pear juice, ½ cup honey, 2 cups flour and ½ cup dried skim milk sifted together. Add the yeast mixture and beat well. Add the ½ cup soft butter, 2 teaspoons salt, 4 beaten eggs, 2 cups chopped pears and the almond flavoring in amount desired. Add 4 cups flour and stir until the dough clears the bowl. Spread the remaining 1 cup flour on the pastry board, turn out dough and knead thoroughly, using a little more flour if necessary. Return to the bowl, brush top of dough with butter, cover and let stand until double in bulk. Turn out, knead lightly, divide and make out into loaves or any desired shapes. Place in greased pans, brush tops with butter, and allow to rise until light. For large loaves, bake in oven preheated to 350° F. for 30 minutes, reduce heat to 325° F. and continue baking for about 25 minutes. This recipe makes 3 large loaves. It is nice to make 1 plain, 1 Bubble Loaf and 1 Cinnamon and Allspice Rolled Loaf.

CHOCOLATE NUT BREAD

1 medium-size cooked potato	¾ cup sugar
Water in which potatoes have been cooked	3 eggs, well beaten
	½ cup cocoa
	4 cups flour
½ cup warm water	1½ teaspoons salt
1 teaspoon sugar	¼ cup soft shortening
¼ teaspoon ginger	1 cup English walnuts,
2 packages dry yeast	chopped
2 cups flour	1 cup flour

(When cooking potatoes for a meal, mash or sieve 1 medium potato and add enough of the potato water to measure 2 cups. Let stand until it is just warm.) Combine the next 4 ingredients and let stand in a warm place until bubbling nicely. In a large bowl stir together the potato mixture, 2 cups flour and ¾ cup sugar. Add the yeast mixture and beat well. Add the 3 well-beaten eggs. Sift together ½ cup cocoa, 4 cups flour, 1½ teaspoons salt and add to ingredients in bowl. Add ¼ cup shortening and 1 cup walnuts, dusting them in the flour mixture before stirring down into the dough. Stir until the dough clears the bowl. Spread 1 cup flour on the pastry board, turn out dough and knead thoroughly until smooth and elastic. Return to bowl, grease top of dough, cover with a towel, and let stand in warm place until double in bulk. Knead lightly, divide, shape into loaves and place in greased pans. Brush tops of loaves with butter and let rise again until light. Bake in oven preheated to 350° F. 45 minutes for medium loaves. This recipe will make 2 medium and 2 small round loaves. It is very nice to make 4 or 5 round sandwich loaves in No. 2½ tin fruit cans. It is also nice when baked in fluted ring molds to glaze when cool with a mixture of 1 cup powdered sugar, 2 tablespoons cream, and ½ teaspoon each of vanilla and brandy flavoring. Sprinkle with toasted, sliced almonds and dot with halves of candied cherries. A delicious sandwich filling for this bread is a combination of cream cheese and finely chopped, candied ginger. It is very nice too, toasted with a topping of whipped butter and honey.

BUBBLE LOAF

Grate or grind enough nuts to make ½ cup. Mix ½ cup sugar with 1 tablespoon cinnamon. Melt ⅓ cup butter. For each loaf make 20 balls of Pear Bread dough about the size of a large walnut. Dip each ball in butter, roll in the sugar mixture and then in the nuts. Place in a generously buttered pan 5 balls to a row and 2 layers deep. Sprinkle remaining sugar and butter over top. Let rise until light and bake as directed above.

CINNAMON AND ALLSPICE ROLLED LOAF

Mix ½ cup sugar, 1 tablespoon cinnamon, 24 coarsely crushed whole allspice, ½ cup finely crushed cereal (such as Grape-Nuts). Roll out ⅓ of the Pear Bread dough about ½-inch thick into an oblong; the width of it being the length of the pan. Spread with melted butter and sprinkle over it evenly the sugar mixture. Roll up as tightly as possible, pinch ends together tightly and place in greased loaf pan. Brush top of loaf with butter, then with a sharp pointed knife, stab almost to the bottom of the loaf at intervals to allow the air to escape from between the layers. Allow to rise until light, bake as directed for plain Pear Bread. Slice and serve warm with butter, or butter slices lightly and toast under broiler to a golden hue to enjoy with the morning coffee.

ITALIAN FRUIT BREAD

½ cup warm water	3 whole eggs
1 teaspoon sugar	3 egg yolks
¼ teaspoon ginger	¾ cup thinly sliced
2 packages dry yeast	candied pineapple
½ cup warm water	¾ cup chopped candied
½ cup sugar	citron
1 cup flour	1 cup golden raisins
½ cup soft butter	4 cups flour
1½ teaspoons salt	

Combine the first 4 ingredients and let stand in a warm place until bubbling nicely. In a large bowl stir together ½ cup warm water, ½ cup sugar and 1 cup flour. Add the yeast mixture and beat well. Add ½ cup butter, 1½ teaspoons salt, 3 whole eggs, 3 egg yolks and mix thoroughly. Dust the fruit with ½ cup flour (taken from the 4 cups measured flour) and add with 2½ cups more of the measured flour to the dough. Stir until the dough clears the bowl. Spread the remaining 1 cup flour on the pastry board, turn out dough and knead well using a little more flour if necessary. Be sure the fruit is well distributed through the dough. Return dough to bowl, brush top with butter, cover and let rise in warm place until double in bulk. Turn out dough, knead well, divide into halves and shape into round loaves. Place in greased 8-inch cake pans, brush tops with butter and let stand in a warm place until double in size. Cut a deep cross or other design on top of each loaf with a very sharp knife. Brush tops with 1 egg white and 1 teaspoon water, beaten until frothy. Bake in oven preheated to 350° F. for 40 to 45 minutes depending upon how dark you wish the crust to be. (Any favorite combination of candied fruit may be used. The addition of 1 tablespoon of grated orange and lemon rind gives a faintly pungent fragrance which is delightful.)

SAFFRON FRUIT BREAD

¼ teaspoon saffron	¾ cup dried skim milk
1 tablespoon warm water	1 cup soft lard
½ cup warm water	3 eggs, well beaten
1 teaspoon sugar	2 teaspoons salt
¼ teaspoon ginger	4 cups flour
2 packages dry yeast	2 cups candied fruit
1½ cups warm water	coarsely chopped
⅞ cup sugar	1 cup flour
2½ cups flour	

Put saffron to soak in 1 tablespoon warm water. Combine the next 4 ingredients and let stand in a warm place until bubbling nicely. In a large bowl stir together 1½ cups warm water, ⅞ cup sugar, 2½ cups flour and ¾ cup dried skim milk. Add the yeast mixture to ingredients in bowl and beat well. Then stir the soaked saffron into the soft lard until the color is even throughout the mixture. Add this, together with 3 eggs, well beaten, and 2 teaspoons salt to the sponge. Add 4 cups flour and 2 cups candied fruit, stirring the fruit into the flour so that it is well dusted before mixing down into the sponge. Stir until the dough clears the bowl. Spread the remaining 1 cup flour on the pastry board, turn out dough and knead well, using a little more flour if necessary. Return to the bowl, grease top of dough, cover and let set in a warm place until double in bulk. Turn out, knead well, divide into even portions, shape into loaves and place in greased pans. Brush tops with soft lard and let rise until light. Place in oven preheated to 400° F. for 15 minutes, reduce heat to 325° F. and bake 45 minutes longer. Brush crust with melted butter and allow to cool in the pans for a few minutes.
(More saffron may be used. Many recipes call for as much as 2 teaspoons, but I suggest that if you are not familiar with saffron you should make your first baking with the smaller amount. The candied fruit should be of the best quality and, for beautiful slices, cut large cherries in halves, pineapple in one-half inch cubes, and other fruits in large pieces.)

APPLE CURRANT LOAF

½ cup warm water
1 teaspoon sugar
¼ teaspoon ginger
2 packages dry yeast
1 cup warm apple juice
½ cup honey
2 cups flour
½ cup dried skim milk
4 tablespoons soft
shortening
1½ teaspoons salt

2 cups dried apples, soaked
drained, chopped
3 cups flour
½ package currants
1 cup flour
4 tablespoons evaporated
milk
4 teaspoons sugar
2 teaspoons nutmeg,
freshly grated

(To prepare the dried apples, cover 1 pound with hot water and let stand overnight. Drain off juice and if there should not be enough, add water to make 1 cup. Cut out any hard places in the apple slices and cut into small bits. This is done easily with a pair of shears. Do not sweeten.)

Combine the first 4 ingredients and let stand in a warm place until bubbling nicely. In a large bowl stir together 1 cup apple juice, ½ cup honey, 2 cups flour and ½ cup skim milk. Add the yeast mixture and beat well. Add 4 tablespoons soft shortening, 1½ teaspoons salt, 2 cups chopped apples, 3 cups flour and ½ package currants. Stir the fruit into the flour until well dusted before mixing down into the sponge. Stir until the dough clears the bowl. Spread 1 cup flour on the pastry board, turn out dough and knead well. This will make quite a stiff dough but additional moisture will be released from the fruit during the baking period. Return to the bowl, grease top of dough, cover and let rise until double in bulk. This will take about 1½ hours. Turn out, knead well and divide dough into 4 equal portions. Form into loaves, place in greased pans, brush tops with butter and let rise until light. Again, this will take about twice as long as for straight dough. When ready for oven, brush tops with evaporated milk, sprinkle with sugar and nutmeg, well mixed together. Bake in oven preheated to 350° F. for the first 15 minutes, reduce heat to 325° F. and continue baking for 40 minutes. Remove from oven and allow loaves to cool for a few minutes with pans turned on their sides, before removing from pans.

ORANGE BREAD

½ cup warm water	2 cups flour
1 teaspoon sugar	2 teaspoons salt
¼ teaspoon ginger	4 tablespoons soft butter
2 packages dry yeast	4 tablespoons grated
½ cup sugar	orange rind
1½ cups warm orange juice	4 cups flour

Combine the first 4 ingredients and let stand in a warm place until bubbling nicely. In a large bowl stir together ½ cup sugar, 1½ cups warm orange juice, and 2 cups flour. Add the yeast mixture and beat well. Add 2 teaspoons salt, 4 tablespoons soft butter, 4 tablespoons grated orange rind, and 3 cups flour. Stir until the dough clears the bowl. Spread the remaining 1 cup flour on the pastry board, turn out dough and knead thoroughly until smooth and elastic. Return to bowl, brush top of dough with butter, cover and let rise until double in bulk. Turn out dough, knead well, divide into equal portions, form into loaves and place in greased pans. Brush tops of loaves with butter, set in warm place and allow to rise until light. Bake in oven preheated to 350° F. for about 45 minutes. Watch carefully as this is a bread that can quickly become too brown. This recipe will make 3 medium-sized loaves.

REMEMBER—*Never use salted nuts in a bread dough. They are fine chopped or ground and sprinkled over the glaze of coffee cakes or rolls, but baked in the dough they become about as appetizing as a rubber band.*

SURPRISE MUFFINS

Using the dough for Orange Bread, pinch off pieces of a size to about half fill a muffin ring when formed into a ball. Press these balls out with fingers into circles about 3 inches in diameter. Place a small spoonful of Orange Marmalade or Pineapple Preserves, or a very soft sweet date folded around a nut meat, in the center of each circle. Draw up the edges of the circles and pinch tightly together. Place balls in muffin rings, pinched side down, brush tops with butter, make a small cross on top of each, cutting down to the filling, so that as the muffins bake, the filling will bubble up a little through the opening. Let rise until very light and bake in oven preheated to 350° F. for about 25 minutes.

REMEMBER—*Look over your spice and seasoning jars every little while to see if there isn't something there that you haven't tried yet in bread. How about a little Chili Powder or a pinch of Nepal Pepper?*

REMEMBER—*If your kitchen is cool, set the bowl of dough on a heavy plate over a bowl of warm water. Never let the outside of the dough bowl become more than comfortably warm to the hand.*

OATMEAL BLACK WALNUT BREAD

1½ cups boiling water
1 cup oatmeal
½ cup warm water
1 teaspoon sugar
¼ teaspoon ginger
2 packages dry yeast
4 tablespoons dark
   brown sugar

2 cups flour
2 tablespoons soft butter
2 teaspoons salt
4 tablespoons light
   molasses
2 cups flour
1 cup black walnut meats
1 cup flour

Pour 1½ cups boiling water over 1 cup oatmeal in a large
bowl and let stand until just comfortably warm. Combine the
next 4 ingredients and let stand in a warm place until bubbling nicely. Add 4 tablespoons brown sugar and 2 cups flour
to the warm oatmeal. Stir well and add the yeast mixture,
beating it in thoroughly. Add 2 tablespoons butter, 2 teaspoons salt, 4 tablespoons molasses, 2 cups flour and 1 cup
black walnuts. Stir the walnuts through the flour until well
coated before mixing down into the dough. Stir until the
dough clears the bowl. Spread the remaining 1 cup of flour
on the pastry board, turn out dough and knead well. Use a
little more flour if necessary to make a stiff dough. This bread
has a coarse texture so that the dough must be stiff or the
loaves will sag in the centers after removal from the oven,
even though well baked. Return dough to the bowl, brush
top with butter, cover and allow to rise until double in bulk.
Turn out, knead well, divide into halves, shape into loaves
and place in well-greased pans. Brush tops of loaves with
butter, cover and allow to rise until double in bulk. Bake in
oven preheated to 375° F. reducing heat to 350° F. after the
first 20 minutes, and continue baking for 25 minutes more.
Remove from oven, turn pans on sides and let cool for a few
minutes before taking loaves from pans.

AUGUSTANA CHRISTMAS BRAIDS (Swedish)

½ cup warm water
1 teaspoon sugar
¼ teaspoon ginger
2 packages dry yeast
1½ cups warm water
½ cup sugar
2 cups flour
½ cup dried skim milk
½ cup soft butter

1 teaspoon salt
2 eggs, well beaten
1 teaspoon powdered
   cardamon
3 cups flour
1 cup white raisins
1 cup candied pineapple,
   chopped
1 cup flour

TOPPING

1 egg white
¾ cup white sugar

1½ cups almonds, sliced
   paper-thin

Combine the first 4 ingredients and let stand in a warm place until bubbling nicely. In a large bowl stir together 1½ cups warm water, ½ cup sugar, 2 cups flour and ½ cup dried skim milk. Add the yeast mixture and beat well. Cover bowl and let stand until this sponge is very light. Add ½ cup soft butter, 1 teaspoon salt, 2 well-beaten eggs, 1 teaspoon cardamon, 1 cup white raisins, 1 cup candied pineapple and 3 cups flour. Stir the fruit around in the flour until well dusted before mixing all down into the sponge. Stir until the dough clears the bowl. Spread the remaining 1 cup flour on the pastry board, turn out dough and knead thoroughly. Return to bowl, brush top of dough with butter, cover and let rise until double in bulk. Turn out dough, knead well, and divide into six equal portions. Shape into long rolls of equal lengths tapered at the ends. Lay 3 rolls together on a greased cookie sheet, braid to each end from the center, pinch ends together and press down tightly to sheet. Brush braid with beaten egg white and sprinkle thickly with sugar and sliced almonds. Let stand in a warm place until light. Bake in oven preheated to 400° F.

for about 25 minutes until well done and the topping is delicately toasted. (This is delightful to serve at a dessert party with a Scandinavian Fruit Soup, either warm or cold, and with plenty of hot coffee.)

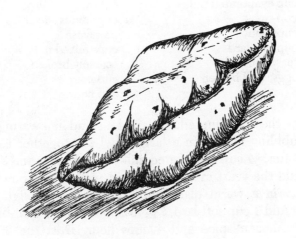

REMEMBER—*Never add chilled ingredients to a yeast bread sponge. In summer use at room temperature, in winter warm slightly such items as raisins, prunes, and other fruits, nuts and grated vegetables.*

CHRISTMAS GIFT BREAD

½ cup warm water
1 teaspoon sugar
¼ teaspoon ginger
3 packages dry yeast
¾ cup warm water
¾ cup evaporated milk
½ cup sugar
3 cups flour
1 cup soft lard
2½ teaspoons salt
4 eggs, well beaten

24 whole allspice, coarsely crushed
4 cups flour
2 cups watermelon preserves, cut into small cubes
2 cups dates sliced crosswise
2 cups mixed nuts, coarsely broken
1 cup flour
1 cup flour

Combine the first 4 ingredients and let stand in a warm place until bubbling nicely. In a large bowl stir together ¾ cup warm water, ¾ cup evaporated milk, ½ cup sugar and 3 cups flour. Add the yeast mixture and beat well. Cover bowl and let stand in a warm place until sponge is very light and bubbly. Add 1 cup soft lard, 2½ teaspoons salt, 4 well-beaten eggs, crushed allspice and 4 cups flour. Dust the 2 cups watermelon preserves, 2 cups dates and 2 cups nuts with 1 cup flour. Add to the rest of the ingredients in the mixing bowl. Stir until the dough clears the bowl. Spread the remaining 1 cup flour on the pastry board, turn out dough and knead thoroughly for several minutes, using a little more flour if necessary. Return to bowl, grease top of dough, cover with towel and let rise until double in bulk. Turn out, knead dough lightly, divide dough into portions and shape into loaves. This recipe will make 6 small oblong loaves in 7x3½x 2½-inch pans. Place loaves in well-greased pans, cover with a barely damp towel, or slip into large plastic bag. (Put tall water glasses between pans to hold plastic up so that it will not rest on top of dough.) Let rise until light, brush tops of loaves with cream or evaporated milk, and sprinkle lightly with sugar and spice if desired. Bake in oven preheated to 350° F. 45 minutes for small loaves, about 60 minutes for large loaves. (These loaves make much appreciated gifts, when attractively wrapped, for Christmas or any other holiday. They improve with age in the freezer.)

SAVARIN (French Dessert) BREAD

½ cup warm water	½ cup dried skim milk
1 teaspoon sugar	¾ cup soft butter
¼ teaspoon ginger	6 eggs, well beaten
2 packages dry yeast	1¼ cups shredded,
¾ cup warm water	blanched almonds
¼ cup sugar	1 teaspoon salt
1 cup flour	3½ cups flour

Combine the first 4 ingredients and let stand in a warm place until bubbling nicely. In a large bowl stir together ¾ cup warm water, ¼ cup sugar, 1 cup flour and ½ cup dried skim milk. Add the yeast mixture and beat well. Cover and let stand until the sponge is very light and bubbly. Beat in ¾ cup soft butter and the 6 eggs, adding the eggs 1 at a time and beating vigorously after each addition. Add 1¼ cups almonds, 1 teaspoon salt and 3½ cups flour. Beat with a large wooden spoon for several minutes. Spoon batter in a very well-oiled large, angel-food tube pan or ring molds. Cover and let stand until double in bulk. Bake in oven preheated to 350° F. for 55 to 60 minutes until well done and delicately brown. Allow to partially cool before removing from pan.

For a dessert guaranteed to make dieters forget to count calories, serve this bread freshly warm or reheated; allow the guests to cut their own slices and take their choice of at least 3 hot syrups—raspberry, apricot and rum are nice—in pitchers to pour over it, frosty whipped cream set in bowl of crushed ice, to spoon on top, and dishes of chopped fresh and toasted nuts, toasted cocoanut and diced candied fruit to sprinkle over it all. Be prepared with an extra pan of Savarin for most of the guests will have to try a slice with each kind of syrup before they are through. These bright clear fruit syrups may be bought in the gourmet sections of the larger food stores, or make them by adding a little hot water to fruit jellies and beat until smooth.

TOMATO JUICE BREAD

½ cup warm water
1 teaspoon sugar
¼ teaspoon ginger
2 packages dry yeast
1½ cups warm tomato
juice
¼ cup sugar
2 cups flour
4 tablespoons soft butter

2 teaspoons salt
or
1 teaspoon salt
½ teaspoon celery salt
½ teaspoon spaghetti Sauce
seasoning (Spice Island
preferred)
4 cups flour

Combine the first 4 ingredients and let stand in a warm place until bubbling nicely. In a large bowl stir together 1½ cups warm tomato juice, ¼ cup sugar and 2 cups flour. Add the yeast mixture and beat well. Add 4 tablespoons soft butter, and the plain salt or the seasoning salt combination. Add 3 cups flour and stir until the dough clears the bowl. Spread the remaining 1 cup of flour on the pastry board, turn out dough and knead thoroughly, using a little more flour if necessary to make a smooth, satiny dough. Return to the bowl, brush top of dough with butter, cover and let rise until double in bulk. Turn out, knead lightly, and form into any desired shapes. This recipe will make 2 standard-size loaves, or about 2 dozen hamburger buns. Place loaves in well greased pan, or buns on greased cookie sheets, brush tops with butter and let rise again until double in bulk. Bake in oven preheated to 350° F., 45 minutes for loaves and about 25 minutes for buns. This dough browns very quickly so it must be watched carefully and the heat adjusted downward if necessary during the second half of the baking period.

(These loaves or buns will be conversation pieces when served at a barbecue. The bright pumpkiny orange color is so attractive, the texture is velvety smooth, and they are so spongy that they never crush when slit with a sharp knife.)

PORK AND ONION BREAD

½ cup warm water	1 cup bacon or fresh side
1 teaspoon sugar	pork, crisply fried,
¼ teaspoon ginger	drained, minced fine
2 packages dry yeast	3 tablespoons minced
2 cups warm water	dried onions
4 tablespoons sugar	1 teaspoon salt
2 cups flour	4 tablespoons soft lard
¾ cup dried skim milk	4 cups flour

Combine the first 4 ingredients and let stand in a warm place until bubbling nicely. In a large bowl stir together 2 cups warm water, 4 tablespoons sugar, 2 cups flour and ¾ cup dried skim milk. Add the yeast mixture and beat well. Add 1 cup minced bacon, 3 tablespoons dried onions, 1 teaspoon salt, 4 tablespoons lard and 3 cups flour. Stir until the dough clears the bowl. Spread the remaining 1 cup flour on the pastry board, turn out dough and knead thoroughly using a little more flour if necessary to make a smooth non-sticky dough. Return to bowl, grease top of dough, cover and let stand in a warm place until double in bulk. Turn out dough, knead lightly and divide into halves for two extra large twisted loaves, or into four equal portions for small loaves. Use two greased cookie sheets, placing one large loaf lengthwise of each sheet, or two small loaves crosswise of each sheet. Slip pans into large plastic bags, or cover lightly with Saran wrap and let rise until light. Brush surface of loaves with 1 egg yolk beaten with 2 tablespoons water. Bake in oven preheated to 350° F. for 20 minutes, reduce heat to 325° F. and continue baking for 25 minutes. Brush with the egg mixture again about 5 minutes before the end of the baking period. For an extra hard crust place pan of boiling water on floor of oven during baking period.

(To make the long twisted loaves, pat portion of dough out into an oval shape about 3 or 4 inches shorter than the baking pan. Have the oval about one-half as wide as it is long and fairly thick in the center. Place on pan, then twist from the center to each end, lifting dough just high enough to turn it over. Press ends down tightly to the pan.)

CARAWAY AND DILL RYE BREAD

½ cup warm water	2 tablespoons caraway seed
1 teaspoon sugar	2 tablespoons dill seed
¼ teaspoon ginger	2 cups rye flour
3 packages dry yeast	3 teaspoons salt
1½ cups warm water	4 tablespoons bacon
½ cup sorghum	drippings
	4 cups white flour

Combine the first 4 ingredients and let stand in a warm place until bubbling nicely. In a large bowl stir together 1½ cups warm water, ½ cup sorghum, 2 tablespoons caraway seed, 2 tablespoons dill seed and 2 cups rye flour. Add the yeast mixture and beat well. Add 3 teaspoons salt, 4 tablespoons bacon drippings, and 3 cups white flour. Stir until the dough clears the bowl. Spread the remaining 1 cup white flour on the pastry board, turn out dough and knead vigorously for several minutes, mound up dough into a ball, and turn bowl upside down over it on the board. Let dough rest for 15 minutes. (It is very important to give the dough this rest period or it will not be possible to work in enough flour to have the loaves hold up properly after rising.) Knead again for several minutes working in all the flour possible to make a very stiff dough. Return to the bowl, grease top of dough, cover with towel, and let rise until double in bulk. Turn out dough, on to board, knead very well and divide into halves. Form each portion into a long taper-loaf. To do this, pound dough out with fist and edge of hand into a thick oblong, fold each side over center, reverse and repeat the process twice. Pinch edges together and lay, seam side down, on an ungreased cookie sheet thickly sprinkled with corn meal. Cover lightly with a thin barely damp towel and allow to rise until light, but not so light that the bubbles begin to burst on the surface. With a sharp knife or scissors make slanting slashes across the tops of the loaves. Brush top with 1 teaspoon Instant Coffee dissolved in 2 tablespoons water. Bake in oven preheated to 350° F. 45 minutes or until the loaves sound hollow when thumped with the fingers.

RUSSIAN ANISE RYE BREAD

½ cup warm water	4 tablespoons soft lard
1 teaspoon sugar	2 teaspoons salt
¼ teaspoon ginger	2 tablespoons dehydrated,
2 packages dry yeast	pulverized orange rind
2 cups warm water	1½ tablespoons anise seed
4 tablespoons dark brown	2 cups rye flour
sugar	3 cups white flour
2 cups rye flour	2 cups seeded raisins
½ cup dried skim milk	1 cup white flour

Combine the first 4 ingredients and let stand in a warm place until bubbling nicely. In a large bowl stir together 2 cups water, 4 tablespoons brown sugar, 2 cups rye flour and ½ cup dried skim milk. Add the yeast mixture and beat well. Add 4 tablespoons lard, 2 teaspoons salt, 2 tablespoons orange rind, 1½ tablespoons anise seed, 2 cups rye flour and 3 cups white flour. Sprinkle 2 cups raisins (be sure that they are plump, soft and well separated) over the flour and stir around until they are well dusted before mixing down into the dough. Stir until the dough clears the bowl. Spreading the remaining 1 cup white flour on the pastry board, turn out dough and knead thoroughly for several minutes. Mound up into a ball on the board, turn bowl over dough and let rest for 15 minutes. Knead again, using more flour if necessary to make a very stiff dough. Return to the bowl, grease top of dough, cover with towel and let rise until double in bulk. Turn out dough, knead lightly, and divide into equal portions. Form into balls for round loaves. This recipe will make 3 medium-sized loaves. Place loaves on cookie sheets, sprinkled generously with corn meal. Slip into large plastic bags, or cover lightly with barely damp towel and let rise until double in bulk. With sharp scissors snip a design on top of each loaf. Brush with cold water, or with 1 teaspoon instant coffee dissolved in a little water, or with milk and bake in oven preheated to 350° F. for 50 to 60 minutes. Loaves should sound hollow when tapped with fingers and the crust should be a deep rich brown.

SWISS SOUR RYE BREAD

½ package dry yeast	1½ tablespoons sugar
½ cup warm water	1½ teaspoons salt
1 cup white flour	2 tablespoons caraway
2 cups warm potato	seed
water	3 cups rye flour
1½ tablespoons sugar	1 cup white flour
3 cups rye flour	

Early in the morning dissolve ½ package dry yeast in ½ cup warm water. Stir in 1 cup white flour. This will be very stiff so it must be covered tightly to keep the top from drying to a crust. Use either a glass or enamel container with fitted lid, or cover a bowl with Saran wrap and fasten down with a rubber band. Let stand in a comfortably warm place until evening of the next day. This mixture is called a "ferment" or "sour dough" and will have a sharply sour smell and taste. On the evening of the second day place this ferment in a very large mixing bowl, add 2 cups warm potato water and stir until well blended. Add 1½ tablespoons sugar and 3 cups rye flour. Beat thoroughly. Cover bowl tightly and let stand in a warm place overnight. This mixture will rise to the top of the bowl in about 3 hours, but will then fall as the sponge is not stiff enough to hold up. In the morning add 1½ table-spoons sugar, 1½ teaspoons salt, 2 tablespoons caraway seed and 3 cups rye flour. Stir to mix as well as possible in the bowl. Spread 1 cup white flour on the pastry board, turn out dough, knead for several minutes until smooth. Mound up into a ball and cover with bowl turned upside down on board. Let rest for 15 minutes. Knead again for several minutes working in all the flour possible, return to bowl, grease top of dough, cover and let rise until double in bulk. Turn out dough, knead lightly, divide into halves, and shape into long tapered loaves. Place on cookie sheet sprinkled generously with corn meal. Let rise until light, covered with a barely damp towel. Brush tops of loaves with 1 teaspoon Postum dissolved in a little hot water. Bake in oven preheated to 325° F. for about 1½ hours, with a pan of boiling water on the floor of the oven during the baking period.

THE KITCHEN

Sometimes I like a kitchen best
When all the work is done,
And it is orderly and sweet.
With fragrance and with sun.
The floor waxed and the curtains crisp.
My apron on its hook—
A kitchen then has such a neat,
Precise, and pleasant look.

But often it seems pleasanter
At five o'clock, I think,
When suddenly it is time to fill
The kettle at the sink,
To start the fire, and lay the cloth
The old familiar way—
Oh, a kitchen is a lovely place
Any time of day!

(Author unknown)

PEASANT'S BLACK BREAD

2 teaspoons Postum
2 cups hot water
4 tablespoons dark
　molasses
2 cups bread crumbs,
　toasted brown and
　finely crushed
½ cup warm water

1 teaspoon sugar
¼ teaspoon ginger
3 packages dry yeast
3 cups rye flour
4 tablespoons bacon
　drippings
2 teaspoons salt
2 cups white flour

Dissolve 2 teaspoons Postum in 2 cups hot water. Add 4 table-spoons molasses and pour over the toasted 2 cups bread crumbs. Let stand until just warm and the crumbs are soaked and soft. Combine the next 4 ingredients and let stand in a warm place until bubbling nicely. Stir yeast mixture into the bread crumb mixture. Add 3 cups rye flour, 4 tablespoons bacon drippings and 2 teaspoons salt. Stir until the dough clears the bowl. Spread 2 cups white flour on the pastry board, turn out dough and knead thoroughly for several minutes, working in as much flour as possible. Turn bowl upside down over the ball of dough on the board and let rest for 15 minutes. Knead again thoroughly, using more flour if necessary to make a very stiff dough. Return to bowl, grease top of dough and let rise until double in bulk. Turn out, knead lightly, divide in halves and shape into either long tapered loaves or regular oblongs for loaf pans. Place on cookie sheets sprinkled thickly with corn meal, or in well-greased loaf pans, sprinkled with meal. Do not grease tops of loaves, but slip into large plastic sacks or cover lightly with Saran wrap and let rise until light. Brush tops of loaves with 1 teaspoon Postum dissolved in 2 teaspoons hot water. Bake in oven preheated to 350° F. 60 minutes, or until well done and quite dry. This bread will have a tendency to draw dampness unless thoroughly baked. (If you bake rye bread regularly, save the end slices and enough crust to toast until dark but not burnt to make the 2 cups of crumbs. Then each time you bake the bread will be darker in color and with more of a parched grain flavor until it resembles the black bread of the old European peasantry. The flavor is wonderful, but anise, dill or caraway seed may be added.

REMEMBER—*Never fill pans too full, give bread room to expand without having to billow out over the sides, causing cracked over-browned crusts and sagging centers of loaves.*

REMEMBER—*Dry coarse bread is caused by insufficient kneading, too much flour, too long a rising period in the pan.*

REMEMBER—*Don't cover baked bread while it is cooling unless you want a soft, slightly damp crust.*

PUMPKIN BREAD

½ cup warm water	½ cup dried skim milk
1 teaspoon sugar	½ cup soft butter
¼ teaspoon ginger	1½ teaspoons salt
2 packages dry yeast	1 teaspoon cinnamon
¾ cup warm water	1 cup cooked sieved
½ cup brown sugar	pumpkin
1 cup flour	4 cups flour

Combine the first 4 ingredients and let stand in a warm place until bubbling nicely. In a large bowl stir together ¾ cup warm water, ½ cup brown sugar, 1 cup flour and ½ cup dried skim milk. Add the yeast mixture and beat well. Add ½ cup soft butter, 1½ teaspoons salt, 1 teaspoon cinnamon, 1 cup pumpkin and 3 cups flour. Stir until the dough clears the bowl. Spread the remaining 1 cup flour on the pastry board, turn out dough and knead thoroughly, using a little more flour if necessary to make a smooth, non-sticky dough. Return to the bowl, grease top of dough with butter, cover and let stand in warm place until double in bulk. Turn out, knead lightly, divide in halves and form into loaves of any desired shapes. This bread makes very nice coiled loaves. To form these, pat out dough to about ⅓ inch thick, 6 inches wide and as long as the portion of dough will reach. Fold the strip in half lengthwise, then with folded edge of strip up roll tightly into a coil. Place in a round flat pudding pan about 2 inches deep and a little larger in diameter than the coil of dough. Brush top of loaves generously with melted butter so that it trickles down into the folds of the coils. Let rise until double in bulk. Bake in oven preheated to 350° F. for about 45 minutes. About 10 minutes before the end of the baking period, brush tops of loaves with evaporated milk so that they will brown to a beautiful russet shade. This recipe will make 2 round coils about 6 inches in diameter.

(Squash or sweet potatoes may be substituted for the pumpkin, but be sure that they are dry and mealy. To prepare, bake in shells or skins, wrapped in aluminum foil, then put through food mill or sieve.)

REMEMBER—*The length of time necessary to allow a dough to double in bulk depends upon temperature, amount of yeast, richness of dough and kind of flour used.*

POLISH BABKA

½ cup warm water	½ cup dried skim milk
1 teaspoon sugar	14 egg yolks
¼ teaspoon ginger	1 teaspoon salt
3 packages dry yeast	4 tablespoons melted butter
1 cup warm water	1 teaspoon almond extract
1 cup sugar	4 cups flour
2 cups flour	½ cup fine rusk crumbs

Combine the first 4 ingredients and let stand in a warm place until bubbling nicely. In a large bowl stir together 1 cup water, 1 cup sugar, 2 cups flour and ½ cup dried skim milk. Add the yeast mixture and beat well. Let stand in a warm place while beating 14 egg yolks with 1 teaspoon salt until very thick and lemon colored. Add to the sponge together with 4 tablespoons butter, 1 teaspoon almond flavoring, and 3 cups flour. Stir until the dough clears the bowl. Spread the remaining 1 cup flour on the pastry board, turn out the dough and knead thoroughly, using a litle more flour if necessary to make a smooth waxy dough. Return to the bowl, brush top of dough with butter, cover and let rise until double in bulk. Turn out, knead lightly and divide into portions according to the size of the pans to be used. Form each portion into a roll long enough to lay around the center of fluted ring molds, filling the molds about ½ full. The ring molds should be thoroughly buttered (this is best done with a pastry brush to be sure all the flutes are coated) and sprinkled thickly with the rusk crumbs. Butter tops of dough rings and sprinkle with crumbs. Let rise until the dough almost fills the molds. Bake in oven preheated to 350° F. for 20 minutes, reduce heat to 325° F. and continue baking 20 minutes longer. This recipe will make 3 rings about 7 inches in diameter.

(For an informal little dessert party feature Babka, either freshly baked or reheated. Allow the guests to cut their own slices. Serve butter, a variety of spreads, dishes of fresh or frozen sugared fruit, a large bowl of creamy cottage cheese with nutmeg, and offer a variety of beverages such as Bouquet of Spice or Jasmine tea, coffee and hot chocolate.)

REMEMBER—*Baking time depends upon size of loaves or rolls and on the temperature used. Slow baking makes a thicker crust, too much sweetening in dough also makes a thicker crust.*

POLISH DOUGHNUTS

2 cups warm water	½ cup sugar
1 teaspoon sugar	½ cup melted butter
¼ teaspoon ginger	1 teaspoon vanilla
2 packages dry yeast	1 tablespoon gated orange
2 cups flour	or lemon rind
4 egg yolks	1 teaspoon salt
1 whole egg	5 cups flour

Combine the first 4 ingredients and let stand in a warm place until bubbling nicely. Beat in 2 cups flour and let stand in warm place to rise for 30 minutes. Beat until very light 4 egg yolks and 1 whole egg. Add to the sponge together with ½ cup sugar, ½ cup melted butter, 1 teaspoon vanilla, 1 table-spoon grated rind, 1 teaspoon salt and 4 cups flour. Stir until the dough clears the bowl. Spread the remaining 1 cup flour on the pastry board, turn out dough and knead thoroughly, using a little more flour if necessary to make a smooth, waxy dough. Return to bowl, grease top of dough, cover and let stand in warm place until double in bulk. Turn out, knead lightly and roll out to ½ inch thickness. Cut with a regular doughnut cutter, or pinch off balls of dough, form into rolls about the thickness of a finger and just long enough to twist into a nice figure 8, pinching the ends tightly together. Lay on lightly floured board or waxed paper, cover lightly with a very thin cloth, and let rise until fairly light. While dough-nuts are rising, put enough lard to heat in a large heavy kettle to make it about 5 to 6 inches in depth. When it reaches the proper temperature (if a thermometer is not available, test heat by dropping cubes of bread into the hot fat. When bread quickly turns a golden brown, the lard is hot enough). Care-fully lift the doughnuts onto a spatula and slide them into the hot lard. Do not fry more than 5 or 6 at a time as it will

reduce the temperature of the lard too much. When doughnuts are golden on both sides, lift out and drain on paper
towels. While still warm roll in sugar. These are perfect for
storing in freezer, tightly wrapped, for they never become
soggy. This recipe will make about 5 dozen large doughnuts.

OLIEKOEKEN (Dutch Batter Balls)

½ cup warm water
1 teaspoon sugar
¼ teaspoon ginger
2 packages dry yeast
1 cup warm water
½ cup sugar
1½ cups flour
½ cup dried skim milk

1 teaspoon salt
½ cup soft butter
3 eggs, well beaten
4 cups flour
Seeded raisins
Candied cherries
Brandy flavoring

Combine the first 4 ingredients and let stand in a warm place until bubbling nicely. In a large bowl stir together 1 cup warm water, ½ cup sugar, 1½ cups flour and ½ cup dried skim milk. Add the yeast mixture and beat well. Add 1 teaspoon salt, ½ cup butter, 3 well-beaten eggs, and 3 cups flour. Stir until the dough clears the bowl. Spread the remaining 1 cup flour on the pastry board, turn out dough, and knead thoroughly until very smooth and satiny. Return to bowl, brush top of dough with butter, cover and let rise in warm place until double in bulk. Turn out dough, knead lightly, pinch off small balls about the size of a large English walnut. Working quickly, mold each piece of dough around 3 or 4 large plump, seeded raisins, or a large candied cherry sprinkled with Brandy flavoring (they should be allowed to stand overnight if possible to soak up the flavoring). Place the dough balls on a sheet of waxed paper, lightly dusted with flour and cover with a sheet of Saran wrap. Allow to rise until very light. While they are rising prepare the fat (I prefer lard) for frying in a deep heavy kettle. It should fill the kettle to a depth of about 5 inches when melted, and is at the right temperature when it browns a cube of white bread to a golden hue very quickly. Transfer the dough balls to spatula or slotted whisk very carefuly so as not to break them open. Slip into the hot fat, frying only 5 or 6 at a time for about 2 minutes until they are a lovely golden brown. Drain on absorbent paper towels and roll in either powdered or granulated sugar while still warm.

CZECH KOLACHKY

½ cup warm water	2 cups flour
1 teaspoon sugar	½ cup dried skim milk
¼ teaspoon ginger	3 eggs, well beaten
2 packages dry yeast	1 teaspoon salt
2 cups warm water	½ cup soft butter
¾ cup sugar	4 cups flour

Combine the first 4 ingredients and let stand in a warm place until bubbling nicely. In a large bowl stir together 2 cups water, ¾ cup sugar, 2 cups flour and ½ cup dried skim milk. Add the yeast mixture and beat well. Add 3 well-beaten eggs, 1 teaspoon salt, ½ cup butter and 3 cups flour. Stir until the dough clears the bowl. Spread the remaining 1 cup flour on the pastry board, turn out dough and knead thoroughly for several minutes, using a little more flour if necessary to make a smooth elastic dough. Return to bowl, brush top of dough with butter, cover with towel and allow to rise until double in bulk. Turn out dough, knead lightly, divide evenly and shape into medium-sized buns. Place on greased cookie sheets far enough apart so that they will not touch when spread out and baked. (A 10½x15-inch sheet will hold 8 buns. Flatten each bun until it is about 3 inches in diameter. Brush tops with melted butter, set in warm place and let rise until about one-half double in bulk. With thumb press dough down in center of each bun forming a well with a ring of dough surrounding it. Fill the depressions with a variety of thick fruit jams or favorite cooked filling. Allow to stand until the buns are very light and puffy. Bake in oven preheated to 350° F. for 25 minutes. As soon as removed from the oven, brush crust around fillings with a thin coating of powdered sugar glaze and sprinkle with paper-thin sliced, toasted almonds.

FILLINGS FOR KOLACHKY

APPLE FILLING—Peel and chop very fine 4 large apples, cook until soft with only enough water to keep from scorching. Add 2 tablespoons cinnamon candies, ⅓ cup sugar and 1 tablespoon lemon juice and cook until thick and clear.

APRICOT FILLING—Steam until very soft ½ lb. dried apricots, add ½ to 1 cup sugar, 1 teaspoon lemon rind and cook until thick. Add 1 to 2 teaspoons rum flavoring if desired.

DATE FILLING—Cook 2 cups of chopped dates with ¼ cup water, a pinch of salt, ⅓ cup brown sugar and ¼ cup butter until thick. Add ½ teaspoon of vanilla or almond flavoring.

FIG FILLING—Cook 2 cups chopped figs until soft with ½ cup water. Add ½ cup sugar, 1 tablespoon lemon rind, a pinch of salt and cook until thick. Stir in ½ cup ground nuts.

POPPY SEED FILLING—Cook 1 cup poppy seed, 2 tablespoons butter, 4 tablespoons honey, 1 cup sugar together over very low heat for 5 minutes, stirring constantly. Add ½ cup finely chopped almonds.

RAISIN NUT FILLING—Cook ½ package of seeded raisins with ½ cup water, ½ cup brown sugar and 1 tablespoon each of lemon and orange rind.

COTTAGE CHEESE FILLING—Mix 1 cup rather dry cottage cheese with 2 well-beaten egg yolks, ⅓ cup sugar, 1 tablespoon lemon rind, 1 tablespoon lemon juice, ½ teaspoon mace and 1 cup finely chopped raisins.

GLAZED BAKED DOUGHNUTS

½ cup warm water
1 teaspoon sugar
¼ teaspoon ginger
2 packages dry yeast
1½ cups warm water
⅓ cup sugar
2 cups flour
½ cup dried skim milk

⅓ cup soft lard
1½ teaspoons salt
2 teaspoons nutmeg
2 teaspoons dehydrated,
  pulverized orange or
  lemon peel
3 eggs, well beaten
3 cups flour

Combine the first 4 ingredients and let stand in a warm place until bubbling nicely. In a large bowl stir together 1½ cups warm water, ⅓ cup sugar, 2 cups flour and ½ cup dried skim milk. Add the yeast mixture and beat well. Add ⅓ cup soft lard, 1½ teaspoons salt, 2 teaspoons nutmeg, 2 teaspoons orange or lemon peel, 3 well-beaten eggs, and 3 cups flour. Beat thoroughly, cover bowl with a barely damp towel and set in warm place to rise until double in bulk. Turn out on floured pastry board and knead lightly. The dough should be only stiff enough to handle. Roll out dough to about ½-inch thickness. Cut into rings with a doughnut cutter. Place on greased cookie sheets. Brush lightly with melted butter and let rise until very light. Bake in oven preheated to 400° F. for 18 to 20 minutes until nicely browned. Dip in hot Glazing Syrup as fast as they are removed from oven and drain on cake racks. (These are perfectly delicious and grand for those people who love doughnuts but cannot eat those fried in deep fat.) This recipe will make about 4 dozen doughnuts.

GLAZING SYRUP—Boil 2 cups sugar and 1 cup water together for about 5 minutes, being careful not to let crystals form. Cover pan for first 2 minutes of boiling period. Add 1 teaspoon lemon juice, stir just enough to blend, and set container in pan of boiling hot water. Dip warm doughnuts quickly and set to drain on racks.

NAZOUK (Persian Tea Bread)

½ cup warm water	3 eggs, well beaten
1 teaspoon sugar	4 cups flour
¼ teaspoon ginger	Filling
2 packages dry yeast	1 cup butter
1 cup warm water	1½ cups sugar
½ cup sugar	3 teaspoons mace
2 cups flour	1½ cups ground Black
½ cup dried skim milk	walnuts
¾ cup soft shortening	1½ cups flour
1 teaspoon salt	

Combine the first 4 ingredients and let stand in a warm place until bubbling nicely. In a large bowl stir together 1 cup water, ½ cup sugar, 2 cups flour and ½ cup dried skim milk. Add the yeast mixture and beat well. Add ¾ cup shortening, 1 teaspoon salt, 3 well-beaten eggs, and 3 cups flour. Stir until the dough clears the bowl. Spread the remaining 1 cup flour on the pastry board, turn out dough and knead thoroughly, using a little more flour if necessary to make a smooth elastic dough. Return to bowl, brush top of dough with butter, cover and let rise until double in bulk. Turn out dough, knead lightly and divide into halves. Roll each portion into an oblong 15 inches wide and about 30 inches long. Lay sheet of dough over a large jelly roll pan (about 11x16 inches), centering ⅓ of the dough in the pan. Spread ¼ of the filling over the dough in the pan. Turn one side section of dough over the center, stretching and fitting to cover filling and press down. Spread second ¼ of filling over this layer of dough. Fold second side section of dough over second layer of filling. Pinch edges of dough tightly together all around oblong. Brush top of dough with melted butter; then, with a very sharp knife cut surface diagonally into 2-inch squares going down through the top layer except at the edges. Repeat same procedure with the second half of the dough. Let rise until double in bulk (because of the heaviness of the filling this will take quite a long time). Place the two pans on racks as near the center of the oven as possible and half way through the baking period reverse their positions. Bake in oven preheated to 350° F. for 45 minutes, reducing the temperature to 325° F. after 20 minutes if it appears that the bread is going to become darker than a biscuit tan by the end of the baking period. About 5 minutes before the end of the baking period, brush the top of the bread thickly with sweetened condensed milk (undiluted). Be sure this has baked to a smooth hard glaze before removing from the oven. Serve either fresh or reheated, broken into diamonds as scored before baking. This sweet bread stores beautifully in freezer for long periods of time. The elusive spicy fragrance improves with age.

TO PREPARE FILLING—Mix the filling ingredients together just like a pastry mix. It is necessary to work with the fingers to make the ingredients bind together. Shape into a roll and divide into fourths. It is best to prepare the filling even before starting the dough, so that it will have as long a time as possible to ripen while the dough is being processed. Do not chill the filling.

SCOT'S CURRANT LOAF (Tea Bread)

½ cup butter	½ teaspoon salt
1½ cup flour	½ teaspoon each of
½ teaspoon salt	cinnamon, mace, allspice
½ teaspoon baking powder	and ginger
Cold water to moisten	½ teaspoon black pepper
1 cup flour	1 cup currants
½ cup sugar	1 cup raisins
½ teaspoon soda	½ cup candied orange peel
½ teaspoon cream of tartar	¾ cup buttermilk

Work ½ cup butter into 1½ cup flour sifted with ½ teaspoon salt and ½ teaspoon baking powder. Mix in enough cold water, about 6 to 8 tablespoons, to make a nice rollable paste. Roll this out as thin as for a regular pie shell. Line a regular loaf pan (9x5x3½ inches), being careful not to punch any holes while fitting dough well into the corners. Roll out an oblong of dough large enough for a cover. Sift together into a large mixing bowl 1 cup flour together with ½ cup sugar and ½ teaspoon each of soda, cream of tartar, salt, cinnamon, mace, allspice, ginger and pepper. Add 1 cup currants, 1 cup raisins and ½ cup candied orange peel. Stir until the fruit is well coated with flour. Add the buttermilk and stir until well blended. Spoon into the lined loaf pan. Lay on the top crust, trim edges and seal neatly to the side edges. Brush with beaten egg thinned with 1 tablespoon milk. Cut a nice design of slots with the point of a sharp knife the length of the top crust. Bake on center shelf of oven preheated to 300° F. for 4 hours. It is best to bake in a heavy glass pan, so that if one sees the side crusts have become as tan as a soda cracker during the first 2 hours of baking, the heat should be reduced to 275° F. for the last 2 hours of the baking period. This makes a very attractive loaf with the outward appearance of a deep dish pie. It should be allowed to stand overnight before cutting, when it makes neat slices of fruit loaf bordered with flaky pastry. A very unusual looking tea bread and simple to make, but people will puzzle over how it is done.

COFFEE CAKE (Basic Recipe)

½ cup warm water	2 cups flour
1 teaspoon sugar	½ cup dried skim milk
¼ teaspoon ginger	2 teaspoons salt
2 packages dry yeast	½ cup soft butter
1½ cups warm water	2 eggs, well beaten
½ cup sugar	5 cups flour

Combine the first 4 ingredients and let stand in a warm place until bubbling nicely. In a large bowl stir together 1½ cups water, ½ cup sugar, 2 cups flour and ½ cup dried skim milk. Add the yeast mixture and beat well. Add 2 teaspoons salt, ½ cup soft butter, 2 well-beaten eggs and 4 cups flour. Stir until the dough clears the bowl. Spread the remaining 1 cup flour on the pastry board, turn out dough, and knead thoroughly using as little flour as possible to make a smooth, non-sticky dough. The dough should only be stiff enough to handle easily. Return to the bowl, brush top of dough with butter, cover with towel, and let rise until double in bulk. Turn out, knead lightly, and make into any one of the delicious coffee cakes for which the directions are given in the following recipes.

REMEMBER—*When bread is doubled in bulk and ready to bake a slight indentation made with the finger will remain.*

HUNGARIAN COFFEE CAKE

Using ½ the dough from the Basic Recipe make into small balls about the size of an English walnut. Have ready a greased 9-inch tube cake pan. Roll each ball in melted butter (it will take about ½ cup) and then in a mixture of ¾ cup white sugar, 2 teaspoons cinnamon and ½ cup fine-ground nuts. Place the balls in layers, with the balls not quite touching in each layer. Sprinkle a few big, plump, seeded raisins, a few slices of candied cherries, and small slivers of bright green candied pineapple between the layers, pressing them into the balls a little. When all the balls have been arranged, scatter any remaining sugar mixture and butter over the top. Cover with a sheet of Saran wrap and let rise until light. Bake in oven preheated to 350° F. for 40 to 45 minutes. Loosen from pan, then let cool a few minutes before turning out.

SWEDISH FRUIT RING

Using ½ of the Basic Coffee Cake dough, roll it out into a rectangle about 9x18 inches. Brush generously with melted butter. Spread with a filling made by mixing together 1 12-ounce jar of Red Raspberry Jam (any other thick fruit jam may be used), ½ cup Grape-Nuts, 2 tablespoons soft butter, and 1 tablespoon grated lemon rind. This is best when mixed before the dough is started so that the Grape-Nuts will have time to soften. Roll up as for a jelly roll. Coil the roll into a circle in a well-greased round cake pan or large pie pan. Brush the top generously with butter, sprinkle with sugar and mace or nutmeg. Cover and let rise until light. Cut down through the dough almost to the bottom at intervals of 2 inches all around the ring so that the filling may bubble up through during the baking. Bake on center rack of oven preheated to 350° F. for about 30 minutes. This is a very good Coffee Cake for storing in the Freezer.

STRUSEL-FILLED COFFEE CAKE

Using ½ of the Basic Coffee Cake dough, divide it into 3 equal portions, pat or roll all three to the same shape to fit what ever square, round or oblong pan you wish to use. Fit the first layer into the well-greased pan, making it as smooth as possible, and sprinkle ⅓ of the Strusel Filling over it. Place the second layer of dough in pan, sprinkle the second ⅓ of the filling over it. Place the third layer of dough in pan and cover with the last portion of filling. Press crumbs slightly down into the dough so that they will stay in place as the dough rises. Cover and let rise until very light. Bake on center rack of oven preheated to 350° F. for 30 minutes.

STRUSEL FILLING

1 cup soft brown sugar, firmly packed	1 tablespoon cinnamon
4 tablespoons butter	4 tablespoons soft butter
	1 cup ground nut meats

Mix well, working up into coarse crumbs to sprinkle between layers and on top of cake.

FRENCH LACED COFFEE CAKE

Using ½ of the Basic Coffee Cake dough, roll it out into a rectangle about 14x9 inches. Place on a well-greased cookie sheet. Spread Walnut Filling down the center of the dough lengthwise, covering the middle 3 inches. Cut each side portion of the dough into 2-inch strips like comb teeth extending out from the filling. Take up a strip from each side, cross them over center of filling. Pull strips down, keeping ends inside, continue lacing opposite strips, pulling them down into a V shape and tucking last ends under. Cover with a sheet of Saran Wrap or a barely damp towel and let rise until very light. Bake on center rack of oven preheated to 350° F. for 30 minutes. Brush generously with sweetened condensed milk about 5 minutes before the end of the baking period, or glaze with 1 cup powdered sugar, 2 tablespoons cream and ½ teaspoon vanilla mixed together, while the cake is still slightly warm.

WALNUT FILLING

1½ cups milk
½ cup sugar
¼ cup honey
2 tablespoons butter
½ teaspoon salt

2 cups walnuts, after grinding
2 whole eggs and 2 egg yolks

Combine all the ingredients except the eggs and bring to the boiling point stirring constantly. Gradually add the well-beaten eggs, and, stirring all the time, cook over very low heat until thick. Cool before spreading on dough.

SCHMIER KASE KUCHEN
(Cottage Cheese Coffee Cake)

Using ¼ of the Basic Coffee Cake dough, pat it into a well-greased 9-inch-round cake pan, forming a rim around the edge so that it is like a pie shell. Fill with the following mixture:

⅓ cup sugar
1 tablespoon flour
½ teaspoon mace
1 teaspoon grated lemon peel

1 cup cottage cheese fairly dry and salted
1 cup drained pineapple cubes

Sprinkle top of filling lightly with sugar and mace or nutmeg. Cover and let rise until light. Bake on center rack of oven preheated to 375° F. for 25 to 30 minutes being sure that the filling is well done. Serve while warm, cutting like a pie into wedge-shaped pieces.

REMEMBER—*The best recipe and the finest ingredients will not insure success if you are not familiar with your oven. Watch your baking every time you try a new recipe.*

EBBEL KUCHEN
(Apple Coffee Cake)

Using ¼ of the Basic Coffee Cake dough, pat it into a well-greased square or oblong layer cake pan, forming a rim around the edges. Brush center and rim generously with melted butter. Sprinkle center with ¼ cup sugar mixed with 1 tablespoon arrowroot or cornstarch and 2 tablespoons cinnamon candies. Cut medium-sized apples (of a good baking variety, such as Jonathan or Winesap), into eighths after peeling, and press into the dough sharp edges down, in neat rows to cover the center depression. Sprinkle top generously with sugar and cinnamon, cover and let rise until very light. Bake in oven preheated to 350° F. for 20 minutes with another pan of the same size inverted over it to be sure that the apples steam and cook (or cover with a sheet of aluminum foil folded down around the edges but not pressed down so that the apples will stick fast). Remove cover and continue baking until nicely browned, increasing the heat to 375° F. if necessary for about 10 minutes longer until nicely browned. Serve while still slightly warm, cut into squares, with coffee, or as a dessert with warm custard sauce.

REMEMBER—*Once you are familiar with the process of baking, use your imagination to experiment with different ingredients and combinations.*

SCOTCH HOT CROSS BUNS

Use the recipe for Basic Coffee Cake dough. At the first kneading divide the dough into halves. Return the first half to bowl, brush top of dough with butter, and let set to rise. To the second half of the dough add:

½ cup white raisins	½ teaspoon nutmeg
1 teaspoon cinnamon	1 teaspoon crushed
2 tablespoons grated	cardamon seed
lemon peel	(optional)
½ cup currants	

Knead until the fruits and spices are well distributed through the dough. Place in a separate bowl, brush top of dough with butter, and set to rise in a comfortably warm place, as it will be slower than the plain dough. When double in bulk turn out, knead lightly, make out into small round buns about 1½ inches across. Place on flat greased pans far enough apart so that they will not touch when light and ready for the oven. Flatten each bun slightly. Now take enough of the plain dough to make a cross for each fruit bun. Roll a small portion of dough between the hands into small pencil-sized rolls. Slash a cross in the top of each bun, just lightly, lay a piece of the little roll in each slash, crossing one over the other and press down slightly. Cover with a sheet of Saran Wrap; let rise in warm place until very light. Bake in oven preheated to 350° F. for 20 minutes. At the end of 15 minutes brush with a little sugar dissolved in a small amount of water. Continue baking until well done, tinged with brown and the syrup has formed a shiny glaze.

SWISS EGG ROLLS

With the remainder of the plain dough from the crosses for the above recipe, make small round buns about 2 inches across, place on greased flat pans far enough apart so that they will not touch when light and ready for the oven. Brush tops lightly with butter, cover with Saran Wrap and let rise until very light. Bake in oven preheated to 350° F. for 20 minutes. At the end of 15 minutes brush with egg yolk beaten with a little water, and bake until the glaze is golden and crisp.

REMEMBER—*A poor job of kneading the dough before the first rising period cannot be remedied.*

REMEMBER—*Never add all the flour the recipe calls for to dough while it is in the bowl. Save ½ or 1 or 2 cups of flour, depending on the size of the recipe, to use while kneading the dough on the pastry board.*

THUMB PRINT COFFEE CAKE

1 cup warm potato water	1 cup warm mashed
1 teaspoon sugar	potatoes
¼ teaspoon ginger	½ cup soft butter
2 packages dry yeast	3 eggs, well beaten
1 cup sugar	1 teaspoon salt
1 cup flour	3 cups flour

Combine the first 4 ingredients in a large bowl and let stand in a warm place until bubbling nicely. Beat in 1 cup sugar and 1 cup flour. Cover and let stand until this sponge is light. Add 1 cup mashed potatoes, ½ cup soft butter, 3 well-beaten eggs, 1 teaspoon salt, and 2 cups flour. Stir until the dough clears the bowl. Spread the remaining 1 cup flour on the pastry board, turn out dough, knead until smooth and satiny, using a little more flour if necessary. The dough should be only stiff enough to work easily. Return to the bowl, grease top of dough, cover and let rise until double in bulk. Knead lightly, roll out to about ¾-inch thickness and fit into shallow, greased pans. Brush tops with melted butter, and let rise until the dough is fairly light and spongy. With the thumb make holes in the dough about 2 inches apart each way. Fill holes with a mixture of melted butter and brown sugar, or any favorite coffee cake filling, sprinkle tops with cinnamon. Let continue rising until very light. Bake in oven preheated to 375° F. for 30 minutes, and the crust is golden brown. This coffee cake is wonderful to serve just as soon as it is cool enough to cut. This recipe will make 2 9x13 inch coffee cakes.

BABAS AU RHUM

½ cup warm water	2 cups flour
1 teaspoon sugar	1 teaspoon salt
¼ teaspoon ginger	4 tablespoons butter
2 packages dry yeast	2 teaspoons rum flavoring
½ cup warm water	1 cup candied fruit, finely
4 tablespoons sugar	chopped
3 eggs, well beaten	2 cups flour

Combine the first 4 ingredients and let stand in a warm place until bubbling nicely. In a large bowl stir together ½ cup warm water, 4 tablespoons sugar, 3 well-beaten eggs, and 2 cups flour. Add the yeast mixture and beat well. Stir in the 1 teaspoon salt, 4 tablespoons butter, and 2 teaspoons rum flavoring. Stir the 1 cup candied fruit (for the fruit use a mixture of lemon and orange peel, pineapple, cherries, and at least 2 tablespoons candied ginger if possible) into the 2 cups flour before stirring into the sponge. Beat all together thoroughly until the fruit is well distributed through the dough. Cover bowl with a damp cloth and let stand in a warm place until the dough is double in bulk. Have ready well-oiled muffin pans with rings for 24. Stir dough down gently and spoon into the muffin rings, filling a little more than ½ full. Brush tops of dough with melted butter, cover again with a barely damp towel, and allow to rise until dough reaches the tops of the rings. Place in center of oven preheated to 350° F. Bake for 25 minutes, watching carefully as the babas should brown only to a light honey color. Brush tops with butter about 5 minutes before the end of the baking period. Remove from rings, place in a large flat pan with sides about 1½ inches deep, and pour over them the Apricot Rum Sauce while it is still very hot. Let stand in a cold place until the sauce is absorbed. It will take at least 3 days for the Babas to be at their mellow best. If you wish to have them ready for use sooner, do not thicken the sauce, but boil the apricot nectar and sugar together for a longer period of time to make it thicker and richer before adding the butter, lemon juice and rum flavoring.

APRICOT RUM SAUCE

1 quart apricot nectar	4 tablespoons butter
1½ cups sugar	juice of 2 lemons
4 tablespoons arrowroot or cornstarch	1 tablespoon, or more, rum flavoring

Boil all together until thickening ingredient is well cooked. Pour over Babas while very hot. This amount of sauce is sufficient for 12 to 15 Babas. Double the amount if the entire baking of 24 is to be used at one time. Serve in individual dessert dishes with a topping of whipped cream or plain vanilla ice cream. (The Babas are ideal for storing in the freezer either before or after they are soaked in the sauce. They may be packaged like muffins or wrapped on individual foil pie pans after they have been soaked in the sauce.)

REMEMBER—*Bread making is a skill, and its results depend upon the cook's deftness in mixing, kneading, letting rise and baking.*

REMEMBER—*Bread is economical because it gives a high return in food value for what it costs.*

REMEMBER—*Don't waste a crumb of bread, for there are endless ways to make use of them in other cooking, and the birds like them too.*

SALLY LUNN

2 cups warm water	½ cup dried skim milk
2 tablespoons sugar	1½ teaspoon salt
¼ teaspoon ginger	2 eggs, well beaten
2 packages dry yeast	4 tablespoons soft butter
2 cups flour	3 cups flour

Combine the first 4 ingredients in a large bowl. Let stand in a warm place until mixture is light and bubbling actively. Beat in 2 cups flour and ½ cup dried skim milk. Add 1½ teaspoons salt, 2 well-beaten eggs, and 4 tablespoons soft butter. Mix well, then add 3 cups flour and beat thoroughly. Cover and let rise until double in bulk. Beat down lightly and spoon into a well-greased 9-inch tube cake pan. Cover and let rise until it is within an inch of the top of the pan. Bake in center of oven preheated to 350° F. for 45 minutes. The crust should be of a golden hue and the top should remain level, not rounded as a loaf of kneaded bread would be. After the first 20 minutes brush crust lightly with butter and brush again about 5 minutes before the end of the baking period. Leave in the pan until partially cooled. This bread is delicious served warm with whipped butter, or when cold, sliced thickly and toasted.

SWEDISH VIENNA BREAD

½ cup warm water	2 cups flour
1 teaspoon sugar	½ cup dried skim milk
¼ teaspoon ginger	1 egg, well beaten
1 package dry yeast	2 cups flour
1 cup warm water	1 cup butter, very cold
2 tablespoons sugar	1 egg

GLAZING

¾ cup powdered sugar	3 tablespoons finely
1½ tablespoons water	shredded candied
	orange peel

Combine the first 4 ingredients and let stand in a warm place until bubbling nicely. In a large bowl stir together 1 cup water, 2 tablespoons sugar, 2 cups flour and ½ cup dried skim milk. Add the yeast mixture and beat well. Add 1 well-beaten egg and 1 cup flour. Stir until the dough clears the bowl. Spread the remaining 1 cup flour on the pastry board, turn out dough, and knead well. Roll out into a square about ½-inch thick. Slice the cold butter, lay between two layers of waxed paper and carefully roll out as nearly as possible to cover center ½ of dough square. Turn edges of dough to center to completely cover butter. Turn one end of oblong thus formed up over center ⅓ of dough, turn other end under center ⅓ of dough. Roll lightly in one direction only to again form an oblong. Again turn one end up over and the other down under. Repeat this process 3 more times and then roll out to about ⅓-inch thick. Cut into 4-inch squares. Turn corners in to center and press down lightly making a smaller square. Place these on lightly-greased cookie sheets, slip into large plastic bags and let stand at room temperature to rise for about 2 hours. The temperature should not be high enough to cause the layers of butter to melt before baking. Brush with whole beaten egg; bake in center of oven preheated to 450° F. for about 12 minutes until golden brown. Glaze as soon as partially cooled.

BASIC SWEET ROLL DOUGH

½ cup warm water	½ cup dried skim milk
1 teaspoon sugar	½ cup soft shortening,
¼ teaspoon ginger	(butter preferred)
2 packages dry yeast	1 teaspoon salt
1 cup warm water	3 eggs, well beaten
8 tablespoons sugar	3 cups flour
2 cups flour	

Combine the first 4 ingredients and let stand in a warm place until bubbling nicely. In a large bowl stir together 1 cup water, 8 tablespoons sugar, 2 cups flour, and ½ cup dried skim milk. Add the yeast mixture and beat well. Add ½ cup soft shortening, 1 teaspoon salt, 3 well-beaten eggs, and 2 cups flour. Stir until the dough clears the bowl. Spread the remaining 1 cup flour on the pastry board, turn out dough and knead well, using only enough flour to make a smooth dough of medium stiffness. (It can now be made up into rolls without a second rising if one wishes to save time, but they will not have the tender, smooth texture that the second rising will produce.) Return dough to bowl, brush top with butter, cover and let rise until double in bulk. Turn out dough, knead lightly, and make out into any kind of rolls desired, let rise until very light and bake as directed for each kind.

REMEMBER—*One can soon learn to tell when bread is ready for the oven by lifting the pan, if it is quite light it is ready, but if it feels heavy it must stand for a longer period.*

GLAZED ORANGE ROLLS

Roll out portions of the Basic Sweet Roll Dough about ¼-inch thick into oblongs about 12x7 inches for each 1 dozen rolls. Spread with Orange Filling; roll as for a jelly roll. Cut into 1-inch slices, place cut side down in greased muffin rings, sprinkle tops lightly with sugar, let rise until very light, and bake in center of oven preheated to 375° F. for about 20 minutes. Remove from pans as quickly as possible after taking from the oven and place top side down on waxed paper until the glaze hardens. If baking 2 pans full at a time, leave second pan in oven with door open while removing rolls from first pan for they stick to pan as soon as they begin to cool.

ORANGE FILLING
Beat together until smooth:

3 tablespoons soft butter	2 tablespoons grated
2 tablespoons orange juice	orange rind
	1½ cup powdered sugar

This amount will be enough filling for 2 dozen rolls.

GLAZED LEMON ROLLS

Proceed as for Glazed Orange Rolls but substitute lemon juice and rind for the orange juice and rind in the filling.

REMEMBER—*Most breads keep perfectly in the freezer if carefully wrapped, so don't be afraid to make up a large recipe.*

GLAZED COFFEE PECAN ROLLS

Prepare Basic Sweet Roll dough as for Glazed Orange Rolls, spread with the following filling, let rise and bake according to directions.

3 tablespoons soft butter	½ cup finely chopped
2 tablespoons evaporated	pecans
milk	1½ cups powdered sugar
1 teaspoon Instant Coffee	

BLUEBERRY ROLLS

Fit small balls of the Basic Sweet Roll dough into muffin rings. With thumb make a depression in center of dough pressing it up on the sides like a tart shell. Put 1 teaspoon thick Blueberry Preserves in the depression. Shape small cap of dough the size of the muffin ring and place over the filling, pushing down lightly around the edges, but not enough to squeeze out the fruit. Brush top generously with butter, sprinkle lightly with sugar and mace. Allow to rise until very light. Bake in center of oven preheated to 375° F. for 20 to 25 minutes. Watch carefully as the rolls should be only lightly browned, but well done so as not to be soggy around the filling. (It is wise to pass the paper napkins with these for they are apt to drip, until one gets used to the right way to hold them, after practicing with several!)

BRIOCHES

½ cup warm water
1 teaspoon sugar
¼ teaspoon ginger
2 packages dry yeast
1 cup warm water
½ cup sugar
2 cups flour
½ cup dried skim milk

⅔ cup soft butter
1 teaspoon salt
5 eggs, well beaten
Grated rind of 1 lemon,
or 2 teaspoons
dehydrated lemon rind
3 cups flour

Combine the first 4 ingredients and let stand in a warm place until bubbling nicely. In a large bowl stir together 1 cup water, ½ cup sugar, 2 cups flour, and ½ cup dried skim milk. Add the yeast mixture and beat well. Add ⅔ cup butter, 1 teaspoon salt, 5 well-beaten eggs, lemon rind, and 2 cups flour. Stir until the dough clears the bowl. Spread the remaining 1 cup of flour on the pastry board, turn out dough, and knead thoroughly using enough flour to make a very smooth, non-sticky but soft dough. Return to bowl, brush top of dough with butter, cover, and let rise until double in bulk. Turn out dough, knead lightly, and shape into brioches. This recipe will make 24. Make smooth balls of dough that will about half fill greased muffin rings when pressed down. Shape a tiny ball of dough, about ¼ the size of the first ones, cut crosswise slits in tops of larger balls, and insert the tiny balls. Brush tops lightly with butter, cover, and let rise until double in bulk. Brush with an egg yolk beaten with a little water, and bake in oven preheated to 350° F. for about 25 minutes until golden brown. Serve either freshly warm or reheated.

(For a truly elegant breakfast bread, make up this recipe in 2 loaves, brioche-shaped just like the individual ones. While warm and just before serving, pour over the loaf a thin glaze of powdered sugar, lemon or orange juice, and soft butter, so that it coats the crown, fills the crease around the base of the crown and drizzles down over the bulging sides of the brioche. Allow the guests to cut their own generous slices with a sharp, serrated knife.)

CARROT ROLLS
(Pennsylvania Dutch)

½ cup warm water
1 teaspoon sugar
¼ teaspoon ginger
2 packages dry yeast
1½ cups potato water
2 tablespoons sugar

1 cup cooked, sieved carrots
2 cups flour
½ cup butter
2 teaspoons salt
2 eggs, well beaten
4 cups flour

Combine the first 4 ingredients and let stand in a warm place until bubbling nicely. In a large bowl stir together 1½ cups potato water, 2 tablespoons sugar, 1 cup carrots, and 2 cups flour. Add the yeast mixture and beat well. Add ½ cup soft butter, 2 teaspoons salt, 2 well-beaten eggs, and 3 cups flour. Stir until the dough clears the bowl. Spread the remaining 1 cup flour on the pastry board, turn out dough and knead thoroughly, using a little more flour if necessary to make a smooth, non-sticky dough. Return to bowl, brush top of dough with butter, cover, and let rise until double in bulk. Turn out, knead lightly, divide and shape into small balls large enough to about ½ fill greased muffin rings, or roll out about ⅓-inch thick, cut into rounds with a biscuit cutter, crease slightly to one side of center, fold over pocket-book like, and place on flat greased pans. Brush tops lightly with butter, and let stand again until very light. Bake in oven preheated to 375° F. for 18 to 20 minutes. After the rolls have baked for 10 minutes, sprinkle tops of rolls quickly with ice water to make them crusty. Serve freshly warm or reheated. Makes about 4 dozen small rolls.

BUTTERMILK ROLLS

½ cup warm buttermilk
1 teaspoon sugar
¼ teaspoon ginger
1 package dry yeast
1½ cups warm buttermilk
2 tablespoons sugar
2 cups flour

1 teaspoon salt
2 tablespoons soft
  shortening
1 cup flour
½ teaspoon soda
1 cup flour

Combine the first 4 ingredients and let stand in a warm place until bubbling nicely. (The buttermilk should be heated to just barely scalding hot, stirring constantly, and cooled immediately to just barely warm to keep it from curdling before using.) In a large bowl stir together 1½ cups warm buttermilk, 2 tablespoons sugar, and 2 cups flour. Add the yeast mixture and beat well. Add 1 teaspoon salt, 2 tablespoons soft shortening and 1 cup flour sifted with ½ teaspoon soda. Stir until the dough clears the bowl. Spread the remaining 1 cup flour on the pastry board, turn out dough and knead well. Do not use more flour unless dough is too sticky to handle. Roll out to ½-inch thickness, and cut into small rounds. Put small cube of butter on one side of center of each round. Turn the other side over and pinch edges together. Place in rows in greased shallow roll pans, brush tops lightly with melted butter, cover lightly and let rise until double in bulk. Bake in center of oven preheated to 375° F. for 20 minutes. Brush tops of rolls with milk and return to the oven for just a minute or two to glaze the crust. This recipe will make about 30 rolls cut with regular-sized biscuit cutter. (These rolls are excellent for storing in the freezer, especially when baked in the shallow disposable aluminum roll pans, so that they need not be removed from the pans for storing. Wrap tightly just as soon as cool to preserve the moisture. Reheat in a very slow oven.)

BUCKWHEAT TEA BUNS

½ cup warm water
1 teaspoon sugar
¼ teaspoon ginger
2 packages dry yeast
1 cup warm water
4 tablespoons light molasses or sorghum
1½ cups buckwheat flour
½ cup dried skim milk

4 tablespoons soft butter
1½ teaspoons salt
4 cups white flour
½ cup ground nuts
½ cup sweetened condensed milk
½ teaspoon vanilla, or Instant Coffee, or a few drops maple flavor

Combine the first 4 ingredients and let stand in a warm place until bubbling nicely. In a large bowl stir together 1 cup water, 4 tablespoons molasses, 1½ cups buckwheat flour, and ½ cup dried skim milk. Add the yeast mixture and beat well. Add 4 tablespoons butter, 1½ teaspoons salt, and 3 cups white flour. Stir until the dough clears the bowl. Spread the remaining 1 cup white flour on the pastry board, turn out dough and knead thoroughly, using a little more flour if necessary to make a smooth elastic dough. Return to the bowl, brush top of dough with butter, cover and let rise until double in bulk. Turn out, knead dough lightly, and shape into small buns. This recipe will make 40 of the right size to bake 8 in each roll pan size 8¾x5¾ inches. Place in well-greased pans, brush tops with butter and allow to rise again until very light. Bake in oven preheated to 350° F. for about 25 minutes. These must be well baked throughout, but only tinged with a soft, rich brown. About 5 minutes before the end of the baking period, put a small amount of the topping of ½ cup ground nuts (filberts are delicious), ½ cup sweetened condensed milk, and the desired flavoring, well mixed, on the center of each bun. Return to the oven and allow the topping to bake until toasted. It will spread a little over the bun as it heats, so a very small mound is all that is needed. (These are best served warm, but are very good cold too. I know of no other bread which causes as much comment, or as many requests for the recipe as this one.)

ENGLISH POPE LADIES

½ cup warm water	½ cup butter
1 teaspoon sugar	1½ teaspoons salt
¼ teaspoon ginger	1½ teaspoons nutmeg
2 packages dry yeast	(or mace)
1 cup warm water	3 eggs, well beaten
⅔ cup sugar	5 cups flour
2 cups flour	Currants
½ cup dried skim milk	1 egg

Combine the first 4 ingredients and let stand in a warm place until bubbling nicely. In a large bowl, stir together 1 cup warm water, ⅔ cup sugar, 2 cups flour, and ½ cup dried skim milk. Add the yeast mixture and beat well. Add ½ cup butter, 1½ teaspoons salt, 1½ teaspoons nutmeg or mace, 3 well-beaten eggs, and 4 cups flour. Stir until the dough clears the bowl. Spread the remaining 1 cup flour on the pastry board, turn out dough, and knead thoroughly, using only as much of the flour as necessary to make a smooth, elastic dough. Return to the bowl, brush top of dough with butter, cover, and let rise until double in bulk. Turn out, knead dough lightly and shape into "ladies." For each body make a fairly flat oval bun about 4 inches long. Place on greased cookie sheets so that they will not touch when the arms are added. For arms, roll pencil-like strips about 4 inches long. Cut in halves crosswise and attach to upper half of oval like "arms akimbo." For the head, make a 1-inch ball of dough and place at top of oval. Flatten just slightly, place a tiny ball of dough in proper position for nose, and use big plump currants for eyes. Slip into large plastic bags and let rise until light. Brush surfaces of ladies with beaten egg, being careful not to displace any of the parts. Bake in oven preheated to 350° F. for about 20 minutes until shiny and tinged with brown. Watch carefully as rolls glazed with beaten egg brown rapidly. This recipe makes 20 ladies. (Children love them and grown-ups are not averse to trying them either.)

IOWA CORN CLOVERS

¼ cup warm water	1½ cups flour
1 teaspoon sugar	½ cup dried skim milk
¼ teaspoon ginger	2 eggs, well beaten
2 packages dry yeast	½ cup soft shortening
1 cup warm water	1½ teaspoons salt
¼ cup sugar	2 cups flour
1 cup yellow corn meal	

Combine the first 4 ingredients and let stand in a warm place until bubbling nicely. In a large bowl stir together 1 cup warm water, ¼ cup sugar, 1 cup yellow corn meal, 1½ cups flour, and ½ cup dried skim milk. Add the yeast mixture and beat well. Add 2 well-beaten eggs, ½ cup soft shortening, 1½ teaspoons salt and 1 cup flour. Stir until the dough clears the bowl. Spread the remaining 1 cup flour on the pastry board, turn out dough and knead thoroughly until smooth and non-sticky. Return to bowl, grease top of dough, cover, and let rise until double in bulk. Knead down dough, shape into very small balls of a size that 4 will about half fill a muffin ring. Have muffin pans ready with the rings well greased, and sprinkled with corn meal. Grease each little ball and place 4 in each ring. Cover and let rise again until very light. Bake in oven preheated to 425° F. for 12 to 15 minutes. Watch carefully as they will become over-brown very quickly. (These light-as-a-feather crunchy rolls go so very well with creamed dried beef gravy, baked potatoes, a bowl of huge juicy onion slices, radishes and celery, and a jar of sharply sweet piccalilli.)

LEMON YEAST BISCUITS

½ cup warm water
1 teaspoon sugar
¼ teaspoon ginger
1 package dry yeast
1 cup warm water
½ cup sugar
2 cups flour
½ cup dried skim milk
1 teaspoon salt

4 tablespoons soft butter
1 whole egg and 1 egg
 white, well beaten
1 tablespoon grated rind
 and zest of lemon
1 teaspoon lemon flavoring
1 cup flour
1 cup plump, soft currants
1 cup flour

Combine the first 4 ingredients and let stand in a warm place until bubbling nicely. In a large bowl stir together 1 cup warm water, ½ cup sugar, 2 cups flour, and ½ cup dried skim milk. Add the yeast mixture and beat well. Add 1 teaspoon salt, 4 tablespoons butter, 1 whole egg and 1 egg white, well beaten, 1 tablespoon lemon rind, 1 teaspoon lemon flavoring, 1 cup flour, and 1 cup currants. Stir currants through flour until well dusted before mixing down into the dough. Stir until the dough clears the bowl. Spread 1 cup flour on the pastry board, turn out dough, and knead thoroughly, using a little more flour if necessary but keeping dough as soft as possible. Return to the bowl, brush top of dough with butter and let rise until double in bulk. Turn out dough, knead lightly, cut into round or diamond shapes, place about 2 inches apart on greased cookie sheets, cover lightly with a very thin cloth, or slip into a large plastic bag. If the bag is large enough so that the end can be tucked under the pan, the air inside will hold it up off the biscuits. Let rise again until double in bulk, brush tops with beaten egg yolk thinned with 2 teaspoons milk. Bake in oven preheated to 400° F. for 18 to 20 minutes. This recipe will make 2 dozen biscuits.

ENGLISH MUFFINS

½ cup warm water
1 teaspoon sugar
¼ teaspoon ginger
1 package dry yeast
1 cup warm water
3 tablespoons sugar
2 cups flour

½ cup dried skim milk
1 egg, well beaten
3 tablespoons soft butter
1½ teaspoons salt
2 cups flour
White corn meal

Combine the first 4 ingredients and let stand in a warm place until bubbling nicely. In a large bowl stir together 1 cup warm water, 3 tablespoons sugar, 2 cups flour, and ½ cup dried skim milk. Add the yeast mixture and beat well. Add 1 well-beaten egg, 3 tablespoons soft butter, 1½ teaspoons salt, and 1 cup flour. Stir until the dough clears the bowl. Spread the remaining 1 cup flour on the pastry board, turn out the dough and knead for about 10 minutes, using a little more flour if necessary, until dough is very smooth and elastic. Return to bowl, brush top of dough with butter, cover with towel and let rise until double in bulk. Turn out carefully onto pastry board, floured only enough to keep dough from sticking. *Do not knead.* Pat out gently, being careful not to break any more air cells than necessary, to almost the desired thickness. Sprinkle top of dough well with white corn meal and roll with pin until proper thickness is reached. For Muffins to be served split and toasted with butter and honey, or jam, ¼-inch thickness is best. For Muffins to be used as shortcakes with fruit, or creamed meat or fish, ½-inch thickness is better. Cut carefully with a sharp 3- to 4-inch cutter. Slip on to sheets of waxed paper sprinkled with corn meal. Cover with a very thin damp cloth and let rise until double in bulk. Bake slowly on ungreased griddle, with temperature a little lower than that used for pancakes. Allow 7 to 8 minutes for browning each side. (These are excellent for storing in freezer and should be wrapped as soon as cool. Never cut with a knife, but split with the tines of a fork.) This recipe will make 12 large muffins.

SALT RISING BREAD

Ferment:

3 medium potatoes
3 tablespoons corn meal,
   yellow or white
1 teaspoon salt

2 tablespoons cold water
4 cups boiling water
1 teaspoon sugar

Dough:

1 cup warm water
½ teaspoon soda
2 cups warm milk
4 cups flour

2 tablespoons soft lard
½ teaspoon salt
10 cups flour

Peel and slice the potatoes into a medium-sized heavy bowl. Moisten 3 tablespoons corn meal and 1 teaspoon salt with 2 tablespoons cold water. Gradually stir in the 4 cups boiling water, being sure that no hard lumps are formed in the meal mixture. Add the 1 teaspoon sugar and pour the boiling hot mixture over the potatoes. Cover the bowl with a heavy plate or flat lid, but use nothing that will rust. Place the bowl in a dishpan or large kettle with boiling water to come as high as possible on the bowl without making it float. Cover the large container with a tight-fitting lid and let it stand in a warm place over night. (I set the dishpan just back of the pilot light on the gas stove.) Early in the morning stir the contents of the bowl. Bubbles should be starting to form on the liquid. Reheat the water around the bowl until it is comfortably warm, never hot. Cover the bowl again until a nice froth of bubbles has formed on top of the liquid. Pour off the liquid into a very large bowl. Rinse the slices of potato with 1 cup warm water. Discard the potatoes. Dissolve ½ teaspoon soda in this 1 cup warm water and add it to the ferment together with 2 cups scalded and cooled milk, and 4 cups flour. Beat vigorously for several minutes. Add 2 tablespoons lard, ½ teaspoon salt and 8 cups flour, 2 cups at a time, beating well after each addition. Spread the remaining 2 cups flour on the pastry board. Turn out dough and knead thoroughly for at least 10 minutes, 15 minutes is better still. The dough will have a very crepey and creamy look, not at all like a commercial yeast dough. Do not use more flour than necessary to keep it from sticking for this should not be a stiff dough. Form into loaves and place in well-greased pans, dusted liberally with corn meal. This recipe will make 5 standard size loaves. These must be kept uniformly and comfortably warm during the rising period. If the pans are warmer on one side than the other, the loaves will rise unevenly. If the weather is cool, it works well to put cookie sheets over pans of warm water, place the bread pans on the sheets and cover with a barely damp cloth. Reheat the water if it becomes too cool. The loaves will not be rounded when light like yeast breads, but flat across the tops. It will take about twice as long as for yeast bread for the loaves to be ready for the oven. Place in oven preheated to 350° F. for 20 minutes, reduce heat to 325° F. and continue baking for another 30 minutes. The tops of the loaves may be lightly dusted with flour or corn meal before baking, or they may be brushed with milk about 5 minutes before the end of the baking period.

(This bread may be stored in the freezer for a long period of time and still be as good as freshly baked bread when reheated. Do slice thinly and wrap very tightly before freezing. There will be a very distinctive odor of fermentation while this bread is being processed, but without it Salt Rising Bread would not have its wonderful taste and texture which make it so pleasing to the people who love it. The final test for any bread is whether it makes good toast. Salt Rising Bread, with its tender crumb and toasty malt flavor, is just made to "go with" homemade jams and jellies.)

OLD-FASHIONED BREAD STARTER

4 medium potatoes	3 tablespoons sugar
1 quart water	1 package dry yeast
2 teaspoons salt	¼ cup warm water

Peel potatoes and cook until tender in 1 quart water. Put potatoes through a food mill or sieve, and add to the water in which they were cooked. Add 2 teaspoons salt and 3 tablespoons sugar. Cool until just warm. Dissolve 1 package dry yeast in ¼ cup warm water and add to the potato mixture. Pour into a 2-quart jar, cover loosely, and let stand at room temperature to rise. Each time the mixture reaches the top of the jar, stir it down. Do this until it stops working. Put lid on jar but do not screw down and store in refrigerator. Use ½ cup of this starter in place of 1 package of dry yeast and ½ cup of water in which the dry yeast would be dissolved. Be sure to stir starter thoroughly in the jar each time before pouring out a portion to use. When the starter has been used down to ½ cup, use this amount in place of the 1 package of dry yeast and ¼ cup water to start a new mix. This starter should be stirred well and a portion of it used 2 or 3 times a week. (In early days neighbors often shared the contents of the starter jar in order to use it regularly to keep it active and renew it often.)

WHITE BREAD (with Starter)

2 cups warm water	2 teaspoons warm water
1 cup Starter	2 tablespoons sugar
½ cup sugar	1½ teaspoons salt
3 cups flour	4 tablespoons soft lard
½ teaspoon ginger	4 cups flour

Combine the first 4 ingredients, beat thoroughly, and let stand in a comfortably warm place, tightly covered, overnight or for several hours until very spongy and light. (I set the covered bowl back of the pilot light on the gas stove.) When the sponge is ready, add ½ teaspoon ginger dissolved in 2 teaspoons warm water, 2 tablespoons sugar, 1½ teaspoons salt, 4 tablespoons soft lard, and 3 cups flour. Stir until the dough clears the bowl. Spread the remaining 1 cup flour on the pastry board, turn out the dough and knead for several minutes, using more flour if necessary to make a smooth elastic dough. (Since the yeast has had two rising periods, once as a starter and once as a sponge, it can now be shaped and placed in the pans, or it can be given an additional rising period before shaping. I prefer the latter method which gives a more even texture.) Divide into portions, shape as desired, place in greased pans, brush tops of loaves or rolls with butter, cover, and allow to stand in a warm place until double in bulk. Bake in oven preheated to 350° F. for about 45 minutes. This recipe will make 3 medium loaves. About 10 minutes before the end of the baking period brush tops of loaves with butter or milk. (Now you have a loaf of real show bread if you have been patient in allowing sufficient time for the rising periods, and have kept the dough uniformly warm. This bread made with Starter and water has a velvety soft crumb that a loaf of milk bread never attains, the crust is delicately crisp but does not crumble badly in slicing, and it has an allover even bisque shade when properly baked, with no cracks, no too-brown spots, or toughness. It will keep fresh much longer and toasts beautifully. From this recipe I like to make 1 loaf, 8 large hamburger buns, and 24 Dutch Strickle Buns.)

DUTCH STRICKLE BUNS

Using a portion of the White Bread with Starter dough, make 24 small round buns about the size of large English walnuts. Place 12 of these in each of 2 well-greased 8x8x1 ¾-inch cake pans. This allows them to double in bulk and still have a little space between the rows. Brush tops of buns with butter. When they are almost double in bulk, trickle the syrup over the buns, dividing it evenly between the 2 pans. Let rise a little longer until very light. Place on lower rack of oven preheated to 350° F. for 15 minutes. Increase heat to 375° F. and transfer pans to top rack of oven for last 15 minutes of baking. The syrup will melt from top of rolls, leaving them nicely glazed and they become only faintly brown. The boiling syrup will coat the bottoms of the rolls and they should not brown at all. Have big plates lightly buttered. Turn rolls upside down on plates quickly as soon as taken from the oven. Some of the syrup will cling to the pans. Scrape it out quickly onto the rolls. If it hardens too fast, hold pan over burner for just a second and it can be easily removed.

SYRUP

1½ cups brown sugar	4 tablespoons boiling water
4 tablespoons butter	1 teaspoon vanilla
4 tablespoons flour	¼ teaspoon maple flavoring

Blend together well and pour over rolls while syrup is still slightly warm. (These taffy-coated buns are popular with young and old alike, and simply melt away. The syrup cooks to a smooth, non-sticky, but not brittle consistency. It seals the little buns in so that they stay as soft and spongy as a fresh marshmallow even when cold. They are wonderful to serve as soon as cool enough to handle with fresh or frozen sugared peaches, liberally sprinkled with lemon juice.)

ELECTION DAY CAKE

½ cup warm water	3 eggs, well beaten
1 teaspoon sugar	1 teaspoon mace
¼ teaspoon ginger	1 teaspoon crushed
2 packages dry yeast	whole allspice
1½ cups warm water	2½ cups flour
¾ cup dark brown sugar	1½ cups raisins
¾ cup white sugar	1 cup drained, cubed
2 cups flour	watermelon preserves
½ cup dried skim milk	or citron
¾ cup soft lard	½ cup flour
1 teaspoon salt	

Combine the first 4 ingredients and let stand in a warm place until bubbling nicely. In a large bowl stir together 1½ cups warm water, ¾ cup dark brown sugar, ¾ cup white sugar, 2 cups flour, and ½ cup dried skim milk. Add the yeast mixture and beat well. Add ¾ cup soft lard, I teaspoon salt, 3 well-beaten eggs, 1 teaspoon mace and 1 teaspoon crushed all-spice. Mix well. Sift 2½ cups flour over the 1½ cups raisins and 1 cup watermelon preserves or citron and mix until the fruit is well dusted with the flour. Add to the rest of the ingredients in the large bowl. Stir until thoroughly mixed. If it is too difficult to do a good job of stirring, spread the remaining ½ cup flour on the pastry board, turn out dough and knead lightly until well mixed. Use no more flour than necessary for this. It will depend upon the amount of moisture in the preserves whether this last ½ cup of flour is needed. Place dough in 2 well-greased loaf pans with the bottoms of pans lined with aluminum foil, also greased. The dough should about half fill the pans. Press well into the corners and against the sides of the pans leaving a slight depression the length of the center of the loaf. Cover pans and let rise until double in bulk. Brush tops of loaves with evaporated milk, sprinkle thickly with sugar and cinnamon, place on center rack of oven preheated to 350° F. and bake about 60 minutes until pressing lightly on the center of the loaf does not leave a depression. Remove from oven, turn pans on sides and let cool for a few minutes before removing from pans. (My mother would have used 1 cup of Old Fashioned Bread Starter beaten with 1 cup flour and 2 tablespoons sugar, and raised to a fine sponge, in place of the 2 packages of dry yeast and added to the 1½ cups warm water (omitting the dried milk, unknown in her days.) Then she would have added a combination of whatever dried and candied fruit she happened to have to make up the 2½ cups of fruit, with possibly a good handful of chopped black walnuts for good measure. She would use whatever spice or combination of spices appealed to her at the moment and the aroma as the "dough cake" baked was enough to draw the men in from the fields. The secret of success with this is to have the dough stiff enough to hold the heavy load of rich fruit when light, but not so stiff that the texture of the loaf is hard and dry when baked.)

RYE NUT BREAD

2 cups white flour	1 cup English walnuts,
1 cup rye flour	chopped
1 teaspoon salt	¼ teaspoon soda
1 tablespoon baking	½ cup light molasses
powder	2 eggs, well beaten
1 teaspoon Instant Coffee	¾ cup undiluted
	evaporated milk

Sift together into a mixing bowl 2 cups white flour, 1 cup rye flour, 1 teaspoon salt, 1 tablespoon baking powder, and 1 teaspoon Instant Coffee. Add 1 cup chopped nuts and dust thoroughly in the flour mixture. Stir ¼ teaspoon soda into ½ cup molasses. Combine with 2 well-beaten eggs and ¾ cup evaporated milk. Blend well and add to the flour mixture in the mixing bowl. Stir until the ingredients are all well-blended together. Have ready a standard size loaf pan well greased, and with the bottom lined with aluminum foil, also well greased. Spoon the batter into the pan, press well into corners and push it a little to sides and ends, leaving a slight depression through center of loaf. Let stand for 15 to 20 minutes to ripen before placing in oven preheated to 350° F. Bake for 1 hour. About 5 minutes before end of the baking period, brush top of loaf with evaporated milk, and brush again as soon as removed from oven. Let bread rest in pan turned on side for a few minutes to cool before removing. It is best to let the bread stand overnight before slicing. Then wrap slices in aluminum foil to reheat, or store in freezer. It improves with age.

GREEK FRUIT BREAD

1 cup dried apricots
1⅓ cup buttermilk
3 tablespoons butter
⅓ cup sugar
2 eggs, well beaten
1½ cups rolled wheat
2 cups flour
2 teaspoons baking
powder
½ teaspoon soda
1 teaspoon salt
1 teaspoon mace

¼ cup blanched almonds
sliced paper thin
¼ cup golden raisins, cut
in halves
1 tablespoon candied
citron chopped fine
1 tablespoon candied
orange peel, chopped
fine
1 tablespoon candied
lemon peel, chopped fine
¼ cup seedless raisins, cut
in halves

Use very soft, tender, waxy apricots. Cut into small pieces and put to soak in 1⅓ cup buttermilk while preparing the rest of the ingredients. Cream 3 tablespoons butter with ⅓ cup sugar. Add 2 well-beaten eggs and cream again until light and fluffy. Add 1½ cups rolled wheat, the apricots and buttermilk, stir well and let stand 15 minutes. Sift 2 cups flour with 2 teaspoons baking powder, ½ teaspoon soda, 1 teaspoon salt and 1 teaspoon mace. Sift 3 tablespoons of this flour mixture over the fruits and nuts; stir until they are separated and well dusted. Add the flour mixture, fruit and nuts to the batter all at once. Stir only until well blended and all the flour is absorbed. Have ready well-greased loaf pans, the bottoms lined with aluminum foil, also well greased. Spoon batter into pans until a little more than half full. This recipe will make 1 large or 2 small loaves. Let stand 15 minutes to ripen. Bake on center rack of oven preheated to 350° F. for about 60 minutes for large loaves, 45 minutes for small loaves. Turn pans on sides and let cool slightly before removing loaves. Let stand overnight before cutting, but wrap tightly as soon as loaves are cool to preserve moisture so that it will not crumble when sliced. (This is a delicious bread to serve either cold, warm or toasted with an assortment of cheeses and plenty of steaming hot coffee or tea.)

HONEY DATE BISCUIT ROLL

3 cups flour	**FILLING**
3 teaspoons baking powder	¼ cup soft butter
3 tablespoons sugar	4 tablespoons honey
1 teaspoon salt	½ cup nut meats, ground
6 tablespoons lard	1 cup dates, thinly sliced
1 cup milk (more or less)	

Sift into a mixing bowl 3 cups of flour, 3 teaspoons baking powder, 3 tablespoons sugar and 1 teaspoon salt. Work in 6 tablespoons lard with fingers as when making pastry. Add about ¾ cup of milk, then add the rest of the cup or a little more to make the dough of the right consistency to roll nicely. Turn dough out on to floured pastry board. Knead only a few times until well bound together. Roll into an oblong about ¼-inch in thickness. Blend ¼ cup soft butter, 4 tablespoons honey and ½ cup nuts together and spread over surface of the dough. Space sliced dates evenly over the surface. Roll tightly as for a jelly roll, cut in about ¾-inch slices, and place cut side down in well-greased pans. Layer cake pans are just right for these rolls. This recipe will make enough for 2 pans with about 10 slices to each. Brush tops of rolls with cream, sprinkle lightly with sugar and a little of a favorite spice if desired. Bake on center rack of oven preheated to 400° F. for about 20 minutes. Watch carefully and adjust heat downward if necessary.

COTTAGE CHEESE BISCUITS

3 cups flour
1 teaspoon salt
2 teaspoons sugar
4 teaspoons baking
    powder
½ teaspoon soda

½ teaspoon cream of tartar
4 tablespoons butter
2 eggs, well beaten
1½ cups cottage cheese,
    small curd
Herbs

Sift together into a large bowl 3 cups flour, 1 teaspoon salt, 2 teaspoons sugar, 4 teaspoons baking powder and ½ teaspoon each soda and cream of tartar. Work in 4 tablespoons butter with fingers until thoroughly blended. Add 2 well-beaten eggs, and 1½ cups cottage cheese. (If cottage cheese is very moist, press out a few spoonfuls of cream before adding to flour mixture. Homemade cheese gives the best results, but can rarely be had.) Stir the mixture just enough to bind together. Turn out on floured pastry board, and knead just enough to make the dough smooth enough to roll. Roll out to the desired thickness, cut out biscuits (I like to cut these in diamond or square shapes so that there will be no scraps to re-roll) and place on ungreased cookie sheets sprinkled with white corn meal. Bake in oven preheated to 425° F. for 10 to 12 minutes. (If these are all to be served hot with a big steaming beef stew, or similar dish, it is very nice to add 1 teaspoon thyme or a combination of herbs to the dough while mixing it. However, if only part of the biscuits are to be used this way and the rest with honey or jelly, do not add the herbs to the biscuit dough, but add them to some whipped butter. Split the number of biscuits desired with a fork as soon as removed from the oven, spread the herb butter on under half, replace tops and return to oven for just a minute before serving.) This recipe will make 18 large biscuits.

QUICK CARAWAY BREAD

3 cups flour	1½ cups water
½ cup dried skim milk	3 eggs, well beaten
½ cup sugar	½ cup flour
1 teaspoon salt	1 cup golden raisins,
3 teaspoons baking	cut in halves
powder	2 tablespoons caraway
4 tablespoons butter	seed

Sift together into a large bowl 3 cups flour, ½ cup dried skim milk, ½ cup sugar, 1 teaspoon salt, and 3 teaspoons baking powder. Work in 4 tablespoons butter with fingers until well blended with flour mixture. Stir in 1½ cups water and 3 well-beaten eggs. Mix well. Sift ½ cup flour over 1 cup golden raisins and stir until well dusted. Add the raisins and 2 tablespoons caraway seed to the batter. Stir until raisins are well distributed through the batter and all flour is absorbed. Have ready 2 medium-sized loaf pans, well greased and dusted with rusk crumbs, or any kind of crisp breakfast cereal, rolled to a fine meal. Spoon batter into prepared pans. Let stand 20 minutes to ripen. Bake on center rack of oven preheated to 350° F. for about 50 minutes. Brush tops of loaves with evaporated milk about 10 minutes before, and again about 5 minutes before the end of the baking period. Turn pans on sides and let cool for a few minutes before removing the loaves. This bread is best when allowed to stand for 24 hours before slicing, but it should be wrapped as soon as cool to preserve moisture. Slice while cold and wrap in aluminum foil to reheat, or toast until nicely browned. The toasted slices are a perfect accompaniment to a fresh fruit salad.

TOASTIN' BISCUITS

3 cups flour	1½ teaspoon salt
3 tablespoons sugar	1 8-ounce package cream
3 teaspoons baking	cheese
powder	3 tablespoons butter
1 teaspoon cream of tartar	2 eggs, well beaten
½ teaspoon soda	½ cup buttermilk

Sift together into a large bowl 3 cups flour, 3 tablespoons sugar, 3 teaspoons baking powder, 1 teaspoon cream of tartar, ½ teaspoon soda, and 1½ teaspoon salt. Work in 1 package cream cheese and 3 tablespoons butter with fingers as though making pastry. Stir in 2 well-beaten eggs and ½ cup buttermilk, lightly beaten together. This will make a very stiff dough. Turn out on lightly floured pastry board. Knead only a few times to make dough handle easily. Roll out to thickness desired, and cut into rounds or any shape preferred. (I like to use a large 3½-inch scalloped cookie cutter, as this very short dough retains the shape of the scallops which are very attractive when baked to a golden brown.) These rise quite high while baking, so for crisply toasted split biscuits, roll to about ¼-inch in thickness. For biscuits to use as a shortcake with fruit, or to serve with creamed fowl or fish, leave sheet of dough about ½-inch thick. Place on ungreased cookie sheets. Bake in oven preheated to 450° F. for about 20 minutes. Watch carefully, for any dough containing cheese browns very quickly. This recipe will make 18 biscuits.

(These biscuits are excellent for storing in the freezer and may be reheated quickly to use in many ways. To split them use a fork, never cut with a knife. To serve with a vegetable salad, spread with herb or garlic seasoned butter before toasting under broiler. To serve with fresh fruit, spread lightly with a brown sugar, butter and cinnamon topping. Watch carefully while toasting so that they do not become too brown).

SPICED MINCEMEAT BREAD

2½ cups flour
3 teaspoons baking powder
½ teaspoon soda
1 teaspoon salt
1 teaspoon cinnamon
1 teaspoon cloves
1 teaspoon allspice
4 tablespoons soft shortening

4 tablespoons brown sugar
2½ cups rolled wheat
2 cups homemade mincemeat
1 cup walnut meats, chopped
½ cup flour
3 eggs, well beaten
½ to ⅔ cup sweet milk

Sift the first 7 ingredients into a large bowl. Work in 4 tablespoons shortening and 4 tablespoons brown sugar. Add 2½ cups rolled wheat. Stir in 2 cups mincemeat and 1 cup chopped nuts dusted with ½ cup flour. Combine 3 well-beaten eggs with ½ cup sweet milk. Pour over other ingredients in bowl and mix thoroughly. If too dry to mix well, add the rest of the milk. The batter will be very stiff. Have ready 2 large loaf pans, well greased, and bottoms lined with aluminum foil also greased. Spoon in the batter, pressing it well into the corners and making the sides a little higher than the centers of the loaves. Allow to ripen for about 20 minutes. Bake on center rack of oven preheated to 350° F. for about 70 minutes. About 5 minutes before the end of the baking period, brush tops of loaves with evaporated milk. Wrap in cellophane as soon as cool but do not slice for 24 hours after baking. This bread keeps indefinitely in the freezer and the flavor improves with age like a fine fruitcake. Be careful to reheat in a very slow oven for breads of this type can become too brown very quickly.

STEAMED BROWN BREAD

2 cups 100% bran	2 teaspoons salt
3 cups buttermilk	2 teaspoons cinnamon
1 cup sorghum	1½ cups seedless raisins
2 cups whole wheat flour	(or seeded, if
2 cups yellow corn meal	preferred)
2 teaspoons soda	2 tablespoons white flour

Soak 2 cups bran in 3 cups buttermilk and 1 cup sorghum for 30 minutes. Add 2 cups whole wheat flour, and 2 cups yellow corn meal sifted with 2 teaspoons soda, 2 teaspoons salt and 2 teaspoons cinnamon. Fold in the raisins dusted with 2 tablespoons white flour. Stir only until well mixed. Have ready 3 No. 2½ tin fruit cans, well greased and the bottoms lined with a circle of aluminum foil. Spoon batter into cans until about ⅔ full. Cover tightly with a double square of foil which is large enough to extend about halfway down on the sides of the cans. Place on a trivet in a large kettle with enough hot water to come up about halfway on the cans. Turn fire low to just keep water bubbling slowly, place lid on kettle and steam for 3 hours. If the kettle lid does not fit properly, check occasionally to be sure that the water stays at the proper level. Add more boiling water if necessary. At the end of the steaming time, take from kettle, remove foil covers from cans and place in oven preheated to 300° F. for 15 minutes. Allow to cool a few minutes before removing rolls from cans. This causes the bread to shrink a little so that it should slide out of the can easily, but run a slim knife around the can first to be sure that the bread is not stuck anywhere. As soon as it is cool, seal tightly in Saran Wrap or cellophane freezer paper to preserve moisture. Store in refrigerator or freezer. When it is to be served; slice with a sharp knife while cold, then rewrap in aluminum foil and heat in slow oven.

STEAMED HONEY DATE BREAD

2 cups rolled wheat	2 teaspoons soda
3 cups buttermilk	2 teaspoons salt
1 cup honey	1½ teaspoons allspice
1 cup rye flour	1 pound dates chopped
1 cup whole wheat flour	2 tablespoons white flour
2 cups white corn meal	

Soak the rolled wheat in 3 cups buttermilk and 1 cup honey for 30 minutes. Add 1 cup rye flour and 1 cup whole-wheat flour. Stir in 2 cups white corn meal sifted with 2 teaspoons soda, 2 teaspoons salt and 1½ teaspoons allspice. Fold in 1 pound chopped dates dusted with 2 tablespoons white flour. Stir only until well mixed. Have ready 3 No. 2½ tin fruit cans, well greased and the bottoms lined with a circle of aluminum foil, also greased. Spoon batter into cans until about ⅔ full. Cover tightly with a double square of foil which is large enough to extend about halfway down on the sides of the cans. Place on a trivet in a large kettle with enough hot water to come up about halfway on the cans. Turn fire low to just keep water bubbling slowly, place lid on kettle and steam for 3 hours. If the kettle lid does not fit tightly, check occasionally to be sure that the water stays at the proper level. Add more boiling water if necessary. At the end of the steaming time, take from kettle, remove foil covers from cans and place in oven preheated to 300° F. for 15 minutes. Allow to cool a few minutes before removing rolls from the cans. This causes the bread to shrink a little so that it should slide out of the can easily, but run a slim knife around the can first to be sure that the bread is not stuck anywhere. As soon as it is cool, seal tightly in Saran Wrap or cellophane freezer paper to preserve moisture. Store in refrigerator or freezer. When it is to be served; slice with a sharp knife while cold, then re-wrap in aluminum foil and heat in a slow oven.

STEAMED MAPLE NUT BREAD

2 cups oatmeal
3 cups buttermilk
1 cup maple syrup
2 cups whole wheat flour
2 cups yellow corn meal
2 teaspoons soda
2 teaspoons salt

1 cup golden muscat raisins
1 cup walnut meats, chopped (English or black)
2 tablespoons white flour

Soak 2 cups oatmeal in 3 cups buttermilk and 1 cup maple syrup for 30 minutes. (If pure maple syrup is not available, use a maple-flavored waffle syrup, or add ½ teaspoon maple flavoring to corn syrup.) Add 2 cups whole-wheat flour and 2 cups yellow corn meal sifted with 2 teaspoons soda and 2 teaspoons salt. Fold in 1 cup raisins and 1 cup nut meats dusted with 2 tablespoons white flour. Stir only until well mixed. Have ready 3 No. 2½ tin fruit cans, well greased and the bottoms lined with circles of aluminum foil, also greased. Spoon batter into cans until about ⅔ full. Cover tightly with a double square of aluminum foil which is large enough to extend about halfway down on the sides of the cans. Place on a trivet in a large kettle with enough hot water to come up about halfway on the cans. Turn fire low to just keep water bubbling slowly, place lid on kettle, check occasionally to be sure that the water stays at the proper level. Add more boiling water if necessary. At the end of the steaming time, take from kettle, remove foil covers from cans, and place in oven preheated to 300° F. for 15 minutes. Allow to cool a few minutes before removing rolls from the cans. This causes the bread to shrink a little so that it should slide out of the can easily, but run a slim knife around the can first to be sure that the bread is not stuck anywhere. As soon as it is cool, seal tightly in Saran Wrap or cellophane freezer paper to preserve moisture. Store in refrigerator or freezer. When it is to be served, slice with a sharp knife while cold, then re-wrap in aluminum foil and heat in slow oven.

REMEMBER—*Use only warm water in which to dissolve yeast, milk only slows the process.*

REMEMBER—*80 to 85 degrees is the ideal temperature range for yeast to grow actively.*

REMEMBER—*Yeast that is allowed to become hot is ruined, discard it. Yeast that is too cool is retarded, warm it and give it sufficient time to grow.*

REMEMBER—*Yeast that is starved for lack of food (sugar and starch) is weakened and cannot be restored to full strength.*

REMEMBER—*Too much sugar also retards the growth of yeast.*

REMEMBER—*To give bread a golden glaze, brush with lightly beaten whole egg just before baking.*

REMEMBER—*For hard, brittle crusts brush surface of bread with water just before baking and place flat pan of water on floor of oven during baking period.*

ADDENDUM

It has now been more than a decade since I first started working seriously on compiling my bread recipes for publication. In that time I have baked thousands of loaves and rolls without ever selling a single one and I still find bread-making as fascinating as I ever did. This, I am sure, is because there is no end to the varieties which can be made, and everyone enjoys creating something new.

The recipes that follow are made by a quick, one-kneading method. Although this might seem traitorous, coming from a long-time baker like me, I realize that many people who love to make bread today (especially those who are career people too) do not have time for two kneadings. While there may be a slight difference in flavor and texture, it is not enough to cause anyone to forego the pleasure of making their own bread because of lack of time.

On working bread twice

For those who *do* have time and want to continue working the dough twice, just turn to the recipe for Perfect White Bread on page 19 and follow the mixing directions for returning dough to mixing bowl for a second period of raising.

About ingredients

It is safe to say that the majority of food items in the markets today can be used in bread. If one has the three basic items—water, leavening agent, and flour of some kind—

bread can be made. Even the leavening agent is not necessary if there is time for preparing a ferment. So it becomes just a matter of how imaginative and ingenious the baker is to tell what the results will be.

Ingredients such as carob powder, unsweetened cocoanut and sunflower seed meal, and oat flour are available from most health-food stores. Interest in these products has grown considerably in the past few years, so I no longer think it necessary to give a list of sources, as I did in *Breads and Coffee Cakes with Homemade Starters,* published by Hearthside in 1967.

BASIC PROCEDURES

A. Mix the dough until it can be worked with the hands and clears the bowl (i.e. does not cling to sides).

B. Turn it out onto board spread with final amount of flour listed.

C. Knead by exerting pressure with heel of palms, lifting and turning as it is worked until smooth and non-sticky. Add small amounts of flour if necessary until this consistency is obtained.

D. If dough is to be given a second kneading, shape into ball, return to bowl, grease top of ball and cover with cloth while resting. If it is a shortening-less dough, instead of greasing top, use a slightly damp cloth for covering.

E. To test readiness for shaping, push fingertips into dough. If dents remain, it is ready to turn out and shape. If dents quickly smooth out, let dough stand a few minutes longer.

F. If, because of a sudden emergency, dough made by the two-kneading method cannot be shaped as soon as it is ready, simply punch down in bowl with two or three sharp blows with the fist. This breaks bubbles, allowing them to divide and increase which encourages fermentation to continue. If it will be more than just a few minutes before it can be placed in the pans for baking, it will be best to set bowl in refrigerator. Allowing dough to stand in warm place after it has become "overlight" weakens the fermentation process so that the finished loaf is inferior in size and texture. (The "punching down" expression comes from the old term "knocking down" the dough used by early professional bakers.)

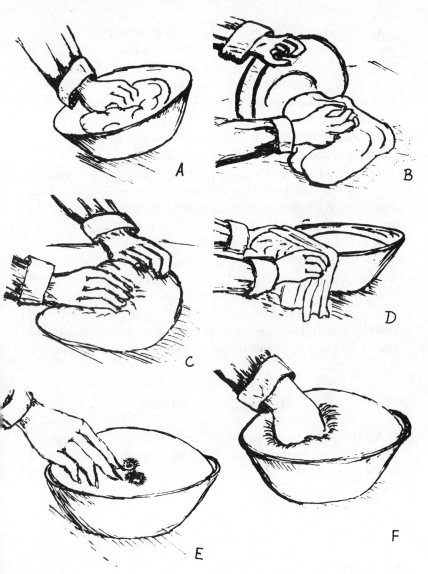

A

B

C

D

E

F

G. Use sharp knife to divide dough into portions for shaping. (For beginners it is a good idea to measure amounts of dough in large measuring cup after dividing, to learn approximately what size portion is right for various sized pans and it soon becomes easy to judge the size of the portions needed.

H. To shape loaf, flatten portion of dough with hands, pushing toward edges with fingers, folded under.

I. Fold flattened dough over double and press down.

J. Stretch and pull, slapping against board if it is a stiff, heavy dough until a long rectangle is obtained with the width equal to the length of pan to be used.

K. Fold over one end and roll up tightly.

L. Place in pan, seam-side down. If not exactly even in height, nudge lightly with fingers until level. For most doughs, the loaf should not fill the pan more than two-thirds full before starting to rise. With very light porous textured breads, half full will be enough to produce a loaf which will round up even with rim of pan before baking.

METHODS OF MIXING

All the yeast bread recipes in first section of book (pages 19 to 123) are made by the traditional two-kneading method while those in the Addendum are made by the time-saving one-kneading method.

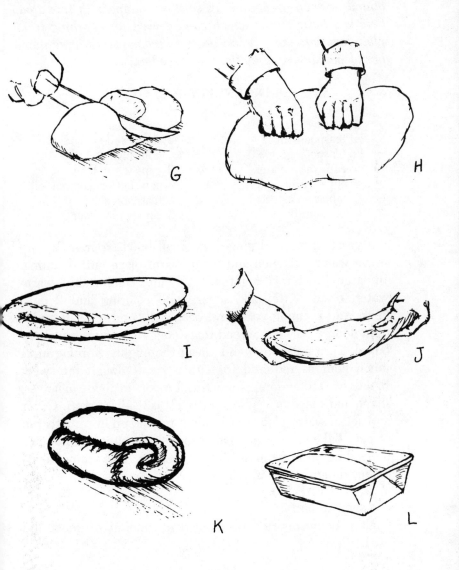

If one needs to make bread in a hurry when supplies are low and there is no time to run to the store, or you're snowbound or even mudbound as so often happens in this area, here is a basic recipe which can be used for anything from plain loaves to the fanciest dessert breads with a large number of possible combinations of ingredients.

INGENUITY BREAD

1 package dry yeast	½ cup sugar
½ teaspoon sugar	4 drops yellow food
¼ teaspoon ginger	coloring
¼ cup warm water	2 cups white flour
1½ cups warm water	¼ cup butter-flavored oil
9 tablespoons dried	1 teaspoon salt
buttermilk	3 cups white flour

Put yeast, sugar and ginger, in small bowl. Pour in ¼ cup warm water. Stir well and set in warm place until foaming. In large bowl mix together 1½ cups comfortably warm water, dried buttermilk, sugar, food coloring and 2 cups flour. Add foaming yeast and beat well. Add oil, salt and 2 cups flour. Mix well. Spread remaining 1 cup flour on pastry board. Turn out dough and knead thoroughly working in as much flour as required for either a soft dough for sweet breads or a stiffer dough for loaves. For loaves divide in halves, shape and place in well-oiled 8½x3½x2½-inch pans. Cover and set in warm place until dough rounds up even with rim of pan. Bake in oven preheated to 350° for 40 to 45 minutes depending on brownness of crust desired. This recipe yields 4 cups dough for 2 large loaves.

FOR SPECIAL DIETS:

—salt may be omitted or equivalent amount of substitute used.

—sweetener in equivalent amount may replace sugar.
—oil may be omitted for fat-free French-type bread.

SUBSTITUTIONS WHICH MAY BE MADE:
—dried buttermilk can be replaced by dried skim milk or coffee creamer in equal amount, or diluted canned milk, homogenized milk or cultured buttermilk in amount equal to water called for or just water alone can be used for a lower-calorie product.
—½ cup white corn syrup or ¼ cup honey may replace sugar.
—an equal amount of any softened shortening may be used in place of the oil.
—the yellow coloring may be omitted and 2 whole beaten eggs added which will require adding about 2 to 4 tablespoons more flour to total amount.
—1 to 1½ cups quick oatmeal or rolled wheat may be used in place of equal amount of white flour.

ELEGANT BUNDT BREAD
(using Ingenuity Dough)

FILLING—PREPARE BEFORE MIXING DOUGH

½ cup white sugar	1 cup ground filberts
4 tablespoons carob powder	½ teaspoon each of vanilla
1 tablespoon cinnamon	and almond extract

Mix all above ingredients together.

ground nuts, bread crumbs	1 recipe Ingenuity Dough
or cocoanut meal	1 stick butter or margarine

Sprinkle a well-buttered bundt pan with ground nuts or bread crumbs or coconut meal. Melt 1 stick of butter or margarine. Prepare the Ingenuity Dough as per preceding recipe. Divide full amount into three pieces of slightly graduated size. Press into strips with fingers wide enough and long enough to lay loosely around tube. Pat the smallest one in place first. Cover with ½ the filling. Dribble almost ½ the butter over the filling. Lay on the next larger strip of dough and repeat with second half of filling and butter. Lay on largest strip. Pat and stretch gently to make top level and smooth. Brush with remaining butter. Cover pan and set in warm place until dough rises to top of tube. Bake in oven preheated to 350° for about 50 minutes (if crust is becoming too .brown lower temperature to 325 for 10 minutes). Remove from oven, allow to cool in pan for 10 minutes. Gently turn out on platter and, while still warm dribble a generous amount of almond- or rum-flavored powdered sugar icing over top so that it will melt enough to run part way down grooves. This is delicious with freshly made applesauce while both are still slightly warm.

SUBSTITUTIONS WHICH MAY BE MADE:

—equal amount of brown sugar may replace white.

—2 tablespoons cocoa may be used in place of carob powder.

—any kind of ground nuts except salted ones may be used instead of filberts.

HAMBURGER LOGS
(using Ingenuity Dough)

¼ portion dough
1 cup prepared chopped
   beef

1 teaspoon minced dried
   onion flakes
Seasoned salt

Brown about ¼ lb. (or two patties) hamburger in skillet with preferred seasoning (as prepared for use in a spaghetti dish). Stir constantly, keeping particles separated as much

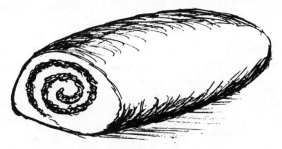

as possible. When nicely browned but not overcooked, remove from heat and tip skillet so excess fat will drain away to one side. Roll ¼ portion dough into rectangle about 12x9 inches. Spread the cooled, finely crumbled hamburger evenly over surface. Sprinkle on the onion flakes and seasoned salt (amount depending upon seasoning used in hamburger). Roll up tightly, starting with the 12-inch side. Place in a long roll pan or on a cookie sheet. Brush top generously with butter and sprinkle lightly with a salad seasoning or paprika, if desired, for a more attractive color. Let stand in warm place until very light. Bake in oven preheated to 350° for 35 to 40 minutes depending on how brown a crust is desired. For a hot main dish, cut into generous slices, lay them in a shallow casserole and pour over a well-seasoned cream gravy made with hamburger fat or use a sauce made from tomato or cream of mushroom soup. Sprinkle top with grated cheese and place under broiler until melted. For a light lunch serve lightly toasted slices with a crisp vegetable salad and assorted cheeses. It also makes very good picnic sandwiches. If one wants fancy-shaped ones, bake the logs in half-circle nut bread pans.

LAST-WORD COFFEE CAKE
(using Ingenuity Dough)

1½ cups dough	½ cup coconut flakes
1 cup chopped dates	2 teaspoons white sugar
Butter	½ teaspoon mace
1 cup finely grated white chocolate	2 tablespoons canned milk

Divide dough in halves and roll into circles to fit into 9-inch layer-cake pan. Place one in well-buttered pan. Sprinkle dates evenly over surface and cover with second round of dough. Brush top generously with butter. Set in warm place until partially raised. Make fairly deep indentations over surface with finger tips. Sprinkle top evenly with the grated chocolate, coconut and last with the sugar and mace thoroughly mixed together. Set in warm place to rise again until very light. Just before placing in oven, dribble a tiny stream of canned milk in whirligig design over topping with lines about 1 inch apart from edge to center. Bake in oven preheated to 350° for 25 to 30 minutes. If topping is browning too fast, reduce heat to 325 after first 15 minutes. (The name was given to this cake by a big "bread eater" the first time he sampled it and he now asks for it every time he comes to visit. It is not for dieters.)

SUBSTITUTIONS WHICH MAY BE MADE:
—raisins, figs or nuts may be used in place of dates.
—sweet chocolate or chocolate bits may be used in place of white but do use white if it can be obtained.
—cinnamon or other favorite spice may be used.
—heavy cream can be used instead of canned milk.

FINNISH VIPURI TWISTS
(using Ingenuity Dough)

Use ½ recipe Ingenuity Dough made by substituting eggs for yellow coloring and adjusting amount of flour as directed under "Substitutions which may be made". Roll out dough into large thin rectangle and sprinkle evenly with ½ teaspoon each of mace (or nutmeg) and powdered cardamon (or 1 teaspoon crushed cardamon). Roll up tightly, then roll and stretch with hands until a good long "rope" with center slightly larger than ends is obtained. Place roll on large greased and floured cookie sheet, curving and twisting into a huge pretzel shape. Brush with boiling water. Let rise until light and brush again with boiling water. Bake in oven preheated to 375° for 40 to 50 minutes until crust is a rich brown. Brush again with boiling water as soon as removed from oven. When cool, transfer to large platter or tray and cut into sections without disturbing shape. Serve with fruit soup. At holiday time it can be served with the open spaces filled with little gingerbread men and other decorated cookies.

DANISH RUM ROLLS
(using Ingenuity Dough)

FILLING—PREPARE BEFORE STARTING DOUGH

2 cups white raisins, ground	1 cup bread crumbs, lightly toasted
½ cup brown sugar	1 egg, beaten
	½ cup rum

Roll ½ portion of dough into rectangle as for making Cinnamon Rolls. Spread with filling. Roll up tightly and cut into slices (up to about 1½ inches thick, depending upon how large a roll is desired). Place on greased cookie sheet, cut-

side up. Brush with milk and sprinkle with sugar. Let stand
until quite light. Bake in oven preheated to 375° for 20 to
25 minutes.

NEAT TRICK CRUNCHIES
(using Ingenuity Dough).

¼ portion dough	Sugar
Chocolate malted milk	Cinnamon
candy balls	12 walnut halves

Divide dough into 12 pieces. Flatten into small circles. Place
1, 2 or even 3 balls (depending on size) in center of each.
Bring edges of circles up and seal over candies. Put sealed side
down in well-buttered muffin tins. Brush tops generously
with butter and sprinkle with sugar and cinnamon. Press a
walnut half into top of each. Let rise in warm place until
very light. Bake in oven preheated to 350° for 20 minutes.
The balls hold their shape very well and make a delicious
crunchy, chewy filling which children all seem to enjoy very
much so that these small muffin-type rolls are perfect for
little birthday parties.

ALL RYE BREAD
(for wheat-free diets)

1 package dry yeast	½ cup brown sugar
½ teaspoon sugar	2 cups rye flour
¼ teaspoon ginger	¼ cup margarine, melted
¼ cup warm water	1½ teaspoons salt
1½ cups warm water	3 eggs, separated
½ cup instant potatoes	½ teaspoon cream of tartar
1 teaspoon instant tea	4 cups rye flour

Put yeast, sugar and ginger in small bowl. Pour in ¼ cup warm water and stir well. Set in warm place until foaming. In large bowl mix together 1½ cups warm water, instant potatoes, tea, brown sugar and 2 cups rye flour. Stir in the foaming yeast and beat well. Add margarine, salt and beaten egg yolks and mix. Add cream of tartar to egg whites and beat until stiff. Add with 3 cups rye flour to dough and stir until well mixed. Spread remaining 1 cup rye flour on pastry board. Turn out dough and knead thoroughly working in as much flour as necessary to make a fairly stiff dough. Cover with bowl and let rest for 10 minutes. Divide dough in halves, shape into loaves and place in well-greased 8½x3½x2½-inch pans. Brush tops with margarine, cover and let set in warm place until dough has rounded up slightly above rim of pans. Have oven preheated to 400°. As soon as loaves are in, reduce temperature to 350° for 20 minutes, then if crust is becoming quite brown reduce temperature again to 325° for remainder of baking period (another 20 to 25 minutes). This bread browns very quickly so should be watched carefully. One doesn't have to be a dieter to enjoy this delicious bread. The crust is chewy but not tough and the texture of the loaf is almost marshmallow soft.

FOR OTHER SPECIAL DIETS:
—salt may be omitted or equivalent amount of salt substitute used.
—brown sugar may be replaced by equivalent amount of low-calorie brown sugar substitute.
SUBSTITUTIONS WHICH MAY BE MADE:
—sorghum or maple-flavored syrup may replace brown sugar.
—butter or bacon fat may be used in place of margarine.

ALMOST-COMPLETE-BREAKFAST BREAD

2 packages dry yeast	1 cup Vanilla Instant
½ teaspoon ginger	Breakfast Mix
1 teaspoon sugar	4 cups white flour
½ cup warm water	½ cup butter-flavored oil
3 cups warm water	2 teaspoons salt
2 teaspoons instant coffee	2½ to 3 cups white flour
2 cups Bran Buds	

Put yeast, ginger and sugar in small bowl. Add ½ cup warm water and mix well. Set in warm place until foaming. In large mixing bowl pour the 3 cups warm water, add instant coffee, Bran Buds, and Instant Breakfast mix. Stir well and let stand until yeast is foaming. Add yeast and beat thoroughly. Beat in 4 cups white flour, the oil and salt. Add 2 cups flour and stir until the dough clears the bowl. Spread remaining flour on pastry board. Turn out dough and knead thoroughly, using a little more flour if necessary to make a good stiff dough. (This bread is quite coarse-textured and raises so light that large loaves will sink in the centers as they cool if the dough is not stiff enough.) Return dough to bowl, brush top with oil, cover and set in warm place until light. It raises very quickly so check its progress sooner than for plain dough. Turn out, divide into portions as desired, knead lightly, shape and place in well oiled pans. Brush tops with oil or butter, cover and let rise until light. Bake in oven preheated to 350° for 40 to 45 minutes for medium loaves. This will make 4 medium loaves. Now all that is needed is butter for the toast and a glass of fruit juice.

FOR SPECIAL DIETS:
—salt may be omitted.

SUBSTITUTIONS WHICH MAY BE MADE:
—other flavors of Instant Breakfast mix.
—soft butter or margarine in place of oil.
—part whole wheat or graham flour in place of white.

APRICOT CURRANT BREAD

1 package dry yeast
½ teaspoon sugar
¼ teaspoon ginger
¼ cup warm water
1½ cups apricot nectar
1 teaspoon apricot brandy essence
½ cup sugar

½ cup dried skim milk
2 cups oat flour
3 eggs, beaten
¼ cup butter-flavored oil
1 teaspoon salt
4 cups white flour
Currants

Put yeast, sugar and ginger in small bowl. Pour in warm water and stir well. Set in warm place until foaming. Heat apricot nectar to just comfortably warm. In large bowl mix it together with the apricot brandy essence, sugar, dried milk and 2 cups oat flour. Add foaming yeast and beat well. Add beaten eggs, oil, salt and 3 cups white flour. Stir until the dough clears the bowl. Spread remaining 1 cup white flour on the pastry board. Turn out dough and knead thoroughly working in as much flour as necessary to make a fairly stiff dough. Divide in halves and roll each portion into a long thin rectangle with the width being equal to the length of the loaf pans. Sprinkle generously with currants. Roll up tightly and place in well-oiled 8½x3½x2½-inch pans. Brush tops with oil, cover and let stand in warm place until dough rounds up slightly above rim of pans. Bake in oven preheated to 350° for 40 to 45 minutes. About 5 minutes before end of baking period, brush tops of loaves with canned milk or cream. This recipe makes 2 loaves.

(Sliced while still slightly warm, or reheated, it is delicious with a bowl of chilled cottage cheese topped with a generous sprinkle of nutmeg.)

FOR SPECIAL DIETS:

—salt may be omitted or replaced with equivalent amount of salt substitute.

SUBSTITUTIONS WHICH MAY BE MADE:

—instant oatmeal may be used in place of the oat flour. This will cause a slight difference in the amount of white flour to be kneaded in to obtain a fairly stiff dough.

BEER BREAD (French Style)

1 package dry yeast	1 tablespoon butter, softened
¼ teaspoon ginger	1 tablespoon salt
½ teaspoon sugar	5 cups white flour
¼ cup warm water	Sesame or poppy seeds
1½ cups beer (12 oz.)	1 egg white
1 tablespoon sugar	

Put yeast, ginger and sugar in small bowl. Add warm water and stir well. Set in warm place until foamy. Heat beer to simmering point only. *Do not* allow to boil. Pour into large bowl, add sugar and when it has cooled to just comfortably warm, stir in 2 cups of the flour. Add the foaming yeast and beat well. Add soft butter, salt and 2 more cups of flour. Stir well. Spread remaining 1 cup of flour on pastry board. Turn out dough and knead thoroughly, working in all the flour and adding just a little more, if necessary to make a very firm dough which can be kneaded vigorously on the unfloured portion of board without sticking. Roll ball in flour, return to bowl, cover and let stand in warm place until doubled in bulk and fingertip dent will remain on surface. Turn out and knead for about 2 minutes again. Divide in halves. Cover and let rest on board for 10 minutes. Shape into long tapered loaves without further kneading by folding in lengthwise from both sides and then flattening by pounding with edge of hand and refolding until loaf is of the length desired.

Gently turn over onto a heavily floured strip and carefully turn back without shaking off flour. Lay side by side lengthwise on slightly greased (or Teflon-coated) cookie sheet which has been sprinkled with cornmeal. Allow as much space as possible between loaves. Cover with sheet of plastic wrap and set in warm place until light enough that fingertip print will remain on surface again. Brush tops with the 1 egg white beaten with 1 tablespoon cold water, being sure all flour coating is moistened. With a very sharp knife make slanted gashes 2 or 3 inches apart the length of the loaf. Sprinkle thickly with sesame or poppy seeds. Put to bake in oven preheated to 375° with a pan of boiling water on floor of oven. After 20 minutes reduce heat to 350° and continue baking 20 to 25 minutes depending on how dark a crust is desired. Prop loaves on edge to cool before slicing. This bread has a marvelous flavor, aroma and texture and freezes perfectly. Do not waste a crumb from slicing but save to use for topping along with a little shredded cheese on vegetable casseroles, escalloped potatoes, etc.

CHESTNUT BANANA BREAD

1 package dry yeast	1 teaspoon vanilla
½ teaspoon sugar	1 teaspoon banana flavoring
¼ teaspoon ginger	½ cup maple-flavored syrup
¼ cup warm water	1 cup dried skim milk
1½ cups warm water	2 cups flour
*1 cup chestnut purée	¼ cup butter, softened
½ cup dehydrated	1 teaspoon salt
banana flakes	3 cups flour

Put dry yeast, sugar and ginger in small bowl. Pour in ¼ cup warm water and stir well. Set in warm place until foaming. In large bowl mix together 1½ cups warm water, chestnut purée, banana flakes, vanilla and banana flavoring, syrup, dried milk and 2 cups flour. Stir in the foaming yeast and beat well. Add the softened butter, salt and 2 cups flour. Stir until the dough clears the bowl. Spread remaining 1 cup flour on the pastry board. Turn out dough and knead thoroughly working in a little more flour if necessary to make a good stiff dough. Divide in halves, shape into loaves and place in well buttered 8½x3½x2½-inch pans. Brush tops with butter, cover and set in warm place until dough rounds up even with rim of pan. Bake in oven preheated to 350° for 40 to 45 minutes. Reduce temperature to 325° after the first 15 minutes. About 5 minutes before end of baking period, brush tops generously with canned milk or rich cream. This recipe makes 2 loaves. (The dough is also perfect for making cinnamon or muffin-type rolls or coffee cakes with any favorite baked on topping.)

* Chestnut purée is very easily made and keeps perfectly in freezer for months. Since it is good for use in so many other ways it is nice to make up a large supply while fresh nuts are in season. After they are peeled, barely cover with water,

cover pan tightly and simmer until tender but not over-cooked. Drain and force through food mill or mash with potato masher and press through sieve. Cool and store in airtight containers in freezer. The purée can also be made from whole canned chestnuts by simmering in liquid from can until tender, then drain and press as above. Already-processed purée is likely to be unsatisfactory because of too much liquid.

This recipe just does not lend itself to changing for any diets for substitutions of any kind would change the unique flavor and quality which results from this combination of ingredients.

COCOANUT CUSTARD BREAD

1 package dry yeast
½ teaspoon sugar
¼ teaspoon ginger
¼ cup warm water
½ cup evaporated milk
½ cup water
1 cup unsweetened cocoanut meal (see page 124)

2 cups flour
½ cup honey
1 to 2 teaspoons cocoanut flavoring
3 eggs, well beaten
½ cup butter
1 teaspoon salt
3 cups flour

Put yeast, sugar and ginger in small bowl. Pour in the warm water. Stir well and set in warm place until foaming. Heat the canned, evaporated milk and ½ cup water until comfortably warm. Pour into large bowl. Add the coconut meal, 2 cups flour, honey and coconut flavoring if desired (depending upon whether just the merest hint of coconut or a distinct flavor and aroma is wanted). Mix all together thoroughly. Add foaming yeast and beat well. Add the well-beaten eggs, softened butter, salt and 2 cups flour. Stir until the dough clears the bowl. Spread remaining 1 cup flour on pastry board. Turn out dough and knead thoroughly working in enough flour to make a fairly stiff dough. Divide in halves, shape into loaves and place in well-buttered 8½x3½x 2½-inch pans. Brush tops generously with butter, cover and set in warm place until dough raises even with rim of pan. Bake in oven preheated to 350° for 40 to 45 minutes. Reduce temperature to 325 after 15 minutes unless a very dark crust is desired as this bread browns very quickly. It has such a rich tender crumb that it is not only good for all kinds of toast, plain, cinnamon or French, but also for all kinds of puddings which use crumbs either as a main ingredient or for toppings.

FOR SPECIAL DIETS:
—salt may be omitted or equivalent amount of substitute used.

SUBSTITUTIONS WHICH MAY BE MADE:
—No substitutions are recommended if the finished product is to live up to the richness suggested by the name.

DATE PUDDING BREAD

2 cups boiling water	¼ cup sugar
2 cups cracked wheat	2 eggs, beaten
1 package dry yeast	¼ cup butter, softened
½ teaspoon sugar	1½ teaspoons salt
¼ teaspoon ginger	2 tablespoons grated
¼ cup warm water	orange rind
1 box (13 oz.) vanilla	2 cups chopped dates
pudding and pie filling	4 cups white flour

(Pour the 2 cups boiling water over cracked wheat. Use brand containing all the wheat germ if possible. Let soak at least 2 hours. Let stand for longer period if a less "crunchy" bread is preferred.)

Put yeast, sugar, and ginger in small bowl. Pour in ¼ cup warm water and mix well. Let set in warm place until foaming. When soaked wheat is ready, reheat it to just warm. In large bowl mix it with the dry pudding (this is the kind which is to be cooked before using as a pudding) and sugar. Add foaming yeast and beat well. Add beaten eggs, soft butter, salt, grated rind, chopped dates and 3 cups white flour. Stir until dough clears the bowl. Spread remaining 1 cup white flour on pastry board. Turn out dough and knead thoroughly, working in enough flour to make a good stiff dough. Divide in halves, shape into loaves and place in well-buttered 8½x3½x2½-inch pans. Brush tops generously with butter, cover and set in warm place until dough has rounded up slightly above rim of pans. Bake in oven preheated to 350° for about 1 hour. Heat may be turned off for last 10 minutes if crust is as brown as desired. This recipe makes 2 large loaves.

It is also nice to divide it into smaller loaves for dainty tea sandwiches, miniature loaves which make welcome gifts especially when glazed with vanilla icing, or for muffins for company breakfasts or luncheons. A delicious date pudding can be made by cutting bread in cubes or stacking slices to make desired amount for individual servings. Place in dishes, spoon on a good warm pudding sauce and, when ready to serve, crown with whipped cream or topping. Not recommended for any dieter except those wishing to gain weight.

SUBSTITUTIONS WHICH MAY BE MADE:
—brown sugar in equal amount may be used in place of white.
—butter may be replaced by margarine or vegetable shortening.
—lemon rind may be used in place of orange.

EGG PASTRY BREAD

5 egg yolks, hard-boiled
1 package dry yeast
½ teaspoon sugar
¼ teaspoon ginger
¼ cup warm water
1½ cups warm water
½ cup dried skim milk

¼ cup sugar
2 cups white flour
2 tablespoons cornstarch
½ cup butter, softened
1 teaspoon salt
3 cups white flour

Prepare egg yolks first and have ready to use before starting to mix dough—place eggs in cold water, bring to boil, cover and simmer 15 minutes. Cool under running water. Peel and remove yolks. Press them through fine wire sieve or food mill. Store whites in refrigerator to use later in salads such as potato or pea or to add to creamed tuna or salmon, etc.

Put yeast, sugar and ginger in small bowl. Pour in ¼ cup warm water and stir well. Set in warm place until foaming. In large bowl mix together 1½ cups warm water, skim milk, sugar, 2 cups white flour and 2 tablespoons cornstarch. Add foaming yeast and mix well. Add sieved egg yolks, soft butter, salt and 2½ cups white flour. Mix well. Spread remaining ½ cup flour on the pastry board. Turn out dough and knead lightly using only enough flour to make the dough stiff enough to roll easily. This will yield 4 cups of basic dough to use as desired in making sweet breads of any kind. If divided in thirds it will make one 9-inch Coffee Round (in layer cake pan) with any favorite topping, 12 plain cinnamon rolls and 12 crescent rolls. A portion may be used to make loaves in miniature pans for tiny sandwiches or bake 2 square buns in each pan with a hidden treat such as a candied cherry, date, etc. in the center of each. Glaze tops of buns with vanilla icing and children will love them. Coffee cakes and rolls should be baked in oven preheated to 350° for about 25 minutes, miniature loaves and buns for 20 to 25 minutes.

EGGNOG HOLIDAY BREAD

1 package dry yeast	2 cups flour
½ teaspoon sugar	2 eggs, beaten
¼ teaspoon ginger	¼ cup butter, softened
¼ cup warm water	2 teaspoons rum flavoring
1½ cups warm water	1½ teaspoons salt
½ cup dry eggnog beads	2 cups Brazil nuts, sliced
1 teaspoon mace	1 cup candied cherries,
½ cup sugar	4 cups flour

(Prepare nuts and cherries before starting to mix dough by cutting crosswise into paper-thin slices. The measurements are for after slicing.)

Put yeast, sugar and ginger in small bowl. Pour in the ¼ cup warm water. Stir well and set in warm place until foaming. In large bowl mix together 1½ cups warm water, eggnog beads, mace, sugar and 2 cups flour. Add foaming yeast and beat well. Add beaten eggs, soft butter, rum flavoring, salt, Brazil nuts, cherries and 3 cups flour. Stir until well mixed. Spread remaining 1 cup flour on pastry board. Turn out dough and knead thoroughly working in enough flour to make a fairly stiff dough. Divide in halves, shape into loaves and place in well-buttered 8½x3½x2½-inch pans. Brush tops generously with butter, cover and set in warm place until dough has rounded up slightly above rim of pans. Bake in oven preheated to 350° for 50 to 55 minutes, reducing the temperature to 325° during last half of baking period so that nuts and fruits in crust will not become too brown. This is such a light, delicately flavored, pretty bread it is appropriate to make at any time of the year, especially if one is in the habit of storing a years' supply of nuts in freezer. For

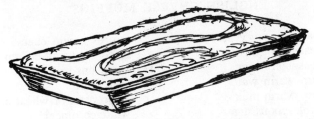

gifts, bake in miniature loaf pans or various sized ring molds and either sprinkle tops before baking with sugar and mace or glaze with powdered sugar icing and decorate after bread has cooled.

Not recommended for any Special Diet except for those who wish to gain weight.

SUBSTITUTIONS WHICH MAY BE MADE:
—½ cup Instant Breakfast powder plus 4 drops yellow food coloring may be substituted for the eggnog beads but, after the first baking, one may want to increase amount of mace and rum flavoring the next time.
—nutmeg may be substituted for mace.
—margarine may be used in place of butter.
—brandy flavoring may be used in place of rum.
—English walnuts may be used in place of Brazil nuts.
—other candied fruit may be used in place of cherries, but be sure that both fruit and nuts are sliced as thin as possible.

ENGLISH CHEESE MUFFINS

1 package dry yeast
¼ teaspoon ginger
½ teaspoon sugar
¼ cup warm water
1 cup warm milk
3 tablespoons sugar
2 cups flour

4 ounces cream cheese
1 large egg, well-beaten
1½ teaspoons salt
2 cups flour
Dry cream of wheat or
white cornmeal

Put yeast, ginger, and sugar in small bowl. Pour in the warm water and stir thoroughly. Set in warm place to rise until foaming. In large bowl mix together the warm milk, 3 tablespoons sugar and 2 cups flour. Stir in yeast mix. Add softened cream cheese, beaten egg and salt. Beat well. Add 1 cup flour and stir until the dough clears the bowl. Spread the remaining 1 cup flour on pastry board. Turn out dough and knead well until all flour is worked in. Coat ball of dough with flour, return to bowl, cover and set in warm place until light. Gently turn out dough on to board floured only enough to keep dough from sticking. *Do not knead.* Pat out gently with hand until almost the desired thickness. Sprinkle top of dough generously with the dry cream of wheat or white cornmeal. Roll very lightly until of the thickness wanted. For muffins to be served toasted with butter and jam for breakfast about ⅓-inch thick is best. For those to be used for shortcakes with fresh fruit and topping or with creamed fish or meat about ⅔ is better. Cut carefully with a sharp 3-inch cutter. Transfer to cookie sheet and sprinkle with the wheat or cornmeal. Cover lightly with sheet of plastic wrap and set in warm place to raise. When doubled in bulk, bake on pancake griddle at temperature a little below that used for pancakes. If not Teflon-coated, rub griddle with oil very lightly. Watch carefully that they do not become too brown.

Bake about 7 minutes on each side, turning very gently. If muffins are to be used fresh, then place in 300° oven for a few minutes until sides are faintly tanned. If they are to be frozen, cool at once. These are excellent for freezing and will keep for a long period of time. The cheese gives them a rich flavor and delicate texture that is much superior to others.

FOR SPECIAL DIETS:

—salt may be omitted.

—an equivalent amount of substitute may be used in place of the sugar but results will not be quite as good.

—low fat cream cheese may be used with no appreciable difference in results.

SUBSTITUTIONS WHICH MAY BE MADE:

—reconstituted dry milk or diluted canned milk may be used.

ENGLISH CRUSTY BREAD

½ cup soft butter	3 large eggs, well-beaten
¾ cup white sugar	3½ cups white flour
2½ cups flaked coconut	2½ teaspoons baking powder
2 tablespoons grated lemon rind	1 teaspoon salt
	1¼ cups milk (about)

Beat butter and sugar together until light and creamy. Add eggs; beat again. Stir in coconut (unpacked measurement) and lemon rind. Sift flour, baking powder and salt together. Add alternately with milk to the batter. If the batter seems too stiff to drop fairly quickly from the spoon, add 1 or 2 more tablespoons of milk. Spoon into well-buttered and floured loaf pans or lined muffin tins and bake in oven preheated to 350° for about 1 hour for loaves, depending upon how brown a crust is desired, and 25 minutes for standard size muffins. This recipe makes 2 high, light loaves in 7½x 3½x2½-inch pans or 2 dozen muffins. The crust is delightfully crunchy. Wonderful to serve with fresh fruit cup for a Sunday brunch are thin buttered slices, lightly sprinkled with sugar and cinnamon or mace, toasted under the broiler and brought to the table piping hot. For an elegant luncheon dessert, lightly toast slices, crumble into sauce dishes and just before serving spoon over chilled vanilla tapioca pudding. Garnish with sugared fresh fruit. This bread freezes well and should be sliced before storing so it is ready for quick use.

FOR SPECIAL DIETS:
—salt may be omitted.

SUBSTITUTIONS WHICH MAY BE MADE:
—margarine for butter.
—unsweetened coconut meal, 2 cups in place of 2½ of flaked coconut. ¼ cup more sugar may be added with this if desired.
—orange rind instead of lemon or a combination of the two.
—an equal amount of reconstituted dry or diluted canned milk in place of whole milk.

JELLY BREAD

1 package dry yeast	2 cups flour
½ teaspoon sugar	2 eggs, beaten
¼ teaspoon ginger	¼ cup butter-flavored oil
¼ cup warm water	1½ teaspoons salt
1 cup hot water	2 teaspoons strawberry
½ cup strawberry jelly	flavoring
½ cup non-dairy cream sub-	3 cups flour
stitute (coffee creamer)	

Put yeast, sugar and ginger in small bowl. Pour in ¼ cup warm water and mix well. Set in warm place until foaming.

Pour 1 cup hot water into 2-cup measure. Add jelly to 1½ cup line. With egg whisk break up jelly and beat until all is dissolved. When mixture is just comfortably warm, pour into large bowl. Mix together with coffee creamer and 2 cups flour. Add foaming yeast and beat well. Add beaten eggs, oil, salt, flavoring and 2½ cups flour. Stir until dough clears the bowl. Spread remaining ½ cup flour on pastry board. Turn out dough and knead thoroughly, using as much flour as necessary to make a smooth, non-sticky, fairly soft dough. Divide in halves, shape into loaves and place in well-oiled 8½x3½x 2½-inch pans. Brush tops with oil, cover and let stand in warm place until dough rounds up slightly above rim of pans. Bake in oven preheated to 350° for 40 to 45 minutes, reducing temperature to 325 for last 15 minutes of baking period if crust is becoming browner than desired. This bread is very white with soft, even texture (could be tinted a delicate pink if desired) and has a delicious, delicate fruit aroma which makes it perfect for using in many ways. (If not using homemade jelly, the aroma may not be as pronounced so one may wish to use more flavoring.) This recipe makes 2 loaves but dough is fine for making any kind of sweet rolls or coffee cakes desired.

To use for individual short cakes, cut still warm or reheated bread into cubes, place in dishes, spoon on chilled strawberries and crown with whipped cream or topping. Allow to stand for a few minutes for bread to absorb juice before serving.

FOR SPECIAL DIETS:
—salt may be omitted or replaced by equivalent amount of substitute.

SUBSTITUTIONS WHICH MAY BE MADE:

—any kind of jelly for which the same kind of fruit flavoring is available may be used.

—coffee creamer may be replaced by dried skim milk or powdered buttermilk in equal amount.

—butter-flavored oil may be replaced by softened butter or margarine in equal amount.

LATIN BROWN BREAD

1 package dry yeast	2 tablespoons vanilla
¼ teaspoon ginger	2 teaspoons instant coffee
½ teaspoon sugar	4 tablespoons sugar
¼ cup warm water	3 cups graham flour
2 cups warm water	¼ cup butter-flavored oil
4 tablespoons coffee creamer (non-dairy cream substitute)	1½ teaspoons salt
	3 cups white flour

Put yeast, sugar and ginger in small bowl. Pour in the ¼ cup warm water and stir well. Set in warm place until foaming. Pour 2 cups warm water into large bowl. Stir in the coffee creamer, vanilla, coffee and sugar. Add graham flour and beat well. Add oil, salt and 2½ cups white flour. Spread remaining ½ cup white flour on pastry board. Turn out dough and knead thoroughly, working in all the flour. Divide in halves, shape into loaves and place in well-greased 8½x 4½x2½-inch pans. Butter tops generously, cover and set in warm place to raise until dough begins to round up slightly above rim of pans. Bake in oven preheated to 350° 45 minutes. About 5 minutes before end of period brush crusts heavily with cream or canned milk.

(Quite often a sack of graham flour has an unpleasant "raw" odor. The vanilla and coffee were added to counteract this and the result was such a delightful rich aroma that the recipe has been used for all graham bread ever since. The loaves, too, are so attractive with the glazed coffee brown crust, I'm sure any woman who bakes bread for sale would find this bread one of her most popular. The name was suggested because both vanilla and coffee come from the Latin American countries.)

FOR SPECIAL DIETS:
—sugar may be replaced by equivalent amount of substitute (there is a tiny amount of sweetening in the coffee creamer).
—salt may be omitted.

SUBSTITUTIONS WHICH MAY BE MADE:

—powdered Instant Breakfast drink may be used in place of coffee creamer.

—butter or margarine may be used in place of oil.

—graham flour may also be used for the 3 cups white flour, which will result in a slightly heavier and slower raising dough.

PINEAPPLE YOGURT BREAD

1 package dry yeast	1 teaspoon pineapple or
½ teaspoon sugar	lemon flavoring
¼ teaspoon ginger	2 cups flour
¼ cup warm water	2 eggs, beaten
1 cup plain yogurt	¼ cup oil, butter-flavored
1 cup crushed pineapple	1 teaspoon salt
unsweetened, undrained	3½ cups flour
½ cup sugar	

Put yeast, sugar and ginger in small bowl. Pour in warm water and stir well. Set in warm place until foaming. Combine yogurt and undrained pineapple. Heat until just comfortably warm. Pour into large bowl. Add ½ cup sugar, flavoring (if desired for a more pronounced flavor and aroma) and 2 cups flour. Mix well. Add the foaming yeast and beat well. Add the well-beaten eggs, oil, salt and 2½ cups flour. Stir until the dough clears the bowl. Spread remaining 1 cup flour on pastry board. Turn out dough and knead thoroughly working in enough flour to make a stiff dough. Divide in halves, shape into loaves and place in well-oiled 8½x3½x2½-inch loaf pans. Brush tops with oil, cover and set in warm place to raise until top of dough is even with rim of pan. Bake in oven preheated to 350° for 40 to 45 minutes. Reduce temperature to 325 after 15 minutes unless a very dark crust is desired, as this bread browns very quickly.

(The ideas for variety breads using this recipe are many. For instance: add ½ cup finely chopped pecans and 1 heaping tablespoon paper-thin tiny chips of candied ginger to one loaf to use for dainty little tea sandwiches put together with whipped cream cheese; or use 1 cup chopped mixed candied fruit and ½ cup chopped nuts for a Fruit Cake type loaf, etc.)

FOR SPECIAL DIETS:
—salt may be omitted or equivalent amount of substitute used.

SUBSTITUTIONS WHICH MAY BE MADE:
—none recommended if product is to retain its special flavor.

RASPBERRY BREAD

½ cup butter	1 teaspoon salt
1 cup white sugar	¾ teaspoon cream of tartar
1 teaspoon rum flavoring	½ teaspoon soda
1 tablespoon lemon juice	1 cup raspberry preserves
4 eggs, unbeaten	½ cup sour cream
3 cups flour	

Cream butter, sugar, flavoring and lemon juice together until light and fluffy. Beat in eggs one at a time until thoroughly mixed. Sift flour with salt, cream of tartar and soda. Stir preserves and sour cream together. Add alternately with the flour to the sugar and egg mix. Stir well. Spoon into two well-buttered and floured 7½x3½x2½-inch loaf pans, or this amount will make 2 dozen muffins in standard size tins. Sprinkle tops with a mixture of 1 tablespoon sugar and ¼ teaspoon mace. Bake in oven preheated to 350° about 45 minutes for loaves, and 25 minutes for muffins.

For party fare, serve tiny sandwiches of this bread thinly sliced and filled with whipped cream cheese and very finely chopped candied ginger. For a Sunday brunch, top muffins with a swirl of cream cheese centered with the delicious little

Swiss Colony red and black raspberry candies which look so much like fresh fruit.

FOR SPECIAL DIETS:
—salt may be omitted.

SUBSTITUTIONS:
—blackberry, strawberry or blueberry preserves may be used instead of the raspberry. Others may be used but do not yield as an attractively colored product.

REALLY RYE

2 packages dry yeast	3 cups rye flour
½ teaspoon ginger	4 eggs, beaten
1 teaspoon sugar	2 teaspoons salt
½ cup warm water	½ cup bacon fat, melted
2 cups warm water	4½ to 5 cups white flour
4 tablespoons sugar	Crisp bacon bits, salad
1 teaspoon instant tea	seasoning, caraway, dill or
1 cup dried skim milk	toasted sesame seeds

Put yeast, ginger and sugar in small bowl. Pour in the ½ cup warm water and stir well. Set in warm place until foaming. Have a large mixing bowl nice and warm. Pour into it the 2 cups warm water. Add the sugar, tea and dry milk. Stir until all is dissolved. Add the rye flour and foaming yeast. Beat well. Add the beaten eggs, salt, bacon fat and 3½ cups white flour. Stir until it clears the bowl. Spread remaining flour on pastry board. Turn out dough and knead well. If necessary add a little more flour to make a smooth, non-sticky dough. Coat ball with flour, return to bowl, cover and set in warm place until light. It is just at the right stage when the ball of dough will roll out of the bowl with just a light nudge or two from the spoon. Without kneading, cut into loaf-size portions. Roll into thin rectangles with the width equal to the length of the loaf pans to be used. Sprinkle each lightly with the bacon bits, salad seasoning or seeds as desired. Roll up and place in well-greased pans. Brush tops with melted fat, cover and set in warm place until light. Bake in oven preheated to 375° for 40 to 50 minutes depending on size of loaves. This will make 4 small loaves and is wonderful for sandwiches, toasting or just for eating fresh and warm with a crisp vegetable salad.

FOR SPECIAL DIETS MAKE THE FOLLOWING SUBSTITUTIONS:
—synthetic sweetener in amount equivalent to sugar.
—salt substitute in amount equivalent to salt.
—butter-flavored oil in same amount as bacon fat.
—only caraway, dill or sesame seeds for seasoning.

(People ask, 'Is this really rye bread?', because the addition of the tea not only lightens and refines the texture but also considerably lightens the color as well. Hence, the origin of the name.)

REUBEN RYE BREAD

1 package dry yeast	½ can Bavarian sauerkraut,
¼ teaspoon ginger	(1 lb. size) undrained
½ teaspoon sugar	2 tablespoons soft bacon fat
¼ cup warm water	1½ teaspoons salt
1 cup warm water	1 tablespoon caraway seed
2 tablespoons sugar	2½ cups white flour
½ cup dry skim milk	Smoke salt seasoning
2 cups rye flour	(optional)

Put dry yeast, ginger and sugar in small bowl. Pour in ¼ cup warm water. Stir well and set in warm place until foaming. In large bowl mix together 1 cup warm water, sugar, dry skim milk and 2 cups rye flour. Add the yeast when ready and beat vigorously. Stir in the sauerkraut, bacon fat, salt, caraway seed and 1½ cups white flour. Spread remaining 1 cup white flour on pastry board. Turn out dough and knead until all flour is worked in. Use a little more if necessary (some cans of sauerkraut contain more juice than others) to make a very, very stiff dough. Turn bowl over ball of dough and let rest for 10 minutes. Divide in halves and shape into loaves. Place in well-greased 8½x4½x2½-inch pans. Grease tops generously with bacon fat and sprinkle very lightly with smoke salt seasoning if desired. Make 4 diagonal slashes across tops. Cover and set in warm place until dough reaches top of pans. Bake in oven preheated to 350° for 45 minutes for loaves, 25 for buns. This recipe makes 2 large loaves or 24 buns.

(With the least amount of effort this bread makes the most appetizing, zesty Reuben sandwiches ever offered with no drippy sauerkraut to make eating a problem. The sandwiches are made with corned beef, sauerkraut, Swiss cheese and rye bread, all toasted or grilled.

Toasted slices or buns are perfect with potato or other vegetable salad, a tray of assorted cheeses and a light dessert for a quick lunch which guests of any station will enjoy.)

SUBSTITUTIONS WHICH MAY BE MADE:

—bacon fat may be replaced with butter, margarine or oil but flavor will suffer slightly.

—dill seed may be used in place of caraway, or a combination of the two is good too.

—1 cup of whole milk may be used in place of dry skim milk

and 1 cup warm water. Homogenized milk need only be heated to comfortably warm.

SAVORY SANDWICH BREAD

1 package dry yeast	½ cup dried skim milk
½ teaspoon sugar	¼ cup sugar
¼ teaspoon ginger	2 cups white flour
¼ cup warm water	¼ cup butter-flavored oil
1½ cups beef consommé (a 10½ oz. can plus water to make full amount)	1 teaspoon seasoned salt
	2 eggs, beaten
	4 cups white flour

Put yeast, sugar and ginger in small bowl. Pour in ¼ cup warm water and stir well. Set in warm place until foaming. Heat consommé to just comfortably warm. In large bowl mix it with skim milk, sugar and 2 cups white flour. Add foaming yeast and beat well. Add oil, seasoned salt, beaten eggs and 3 cups white flour. Stir until dough clears the bowl. Spread remaining 1 cup white flour on pastry board. Turn out dough and knead thoroughly, working in enough flour to make a smooth, non-sticky dough. Divide in halves, shape into loaves, brush tops with oil, cover and set in warm place until dough rounds up a little above rim of pans. Bake in oven preheated to 350° for 40 to 45 minutes. If browning too quickly, reduce temperature to 325 for last half of baking period.

This recipe makes 2 high, light loaves which can't be topped for making sandwiches with lettuce and sliced tomatoes or any favorite vegetable or meat filling.

The full amount of dough will make 2 to 2½ doz. light, puffy hamburger buns and for Dried Beef Roll-ups, roll ¼ portions of dough into about 12-inch circles, cut into 8 equal wedges and lay 2 paper-thin rounds of dried beef on wide ends. Stretching dough to completely cover meat, roll up tightly. Lay on oiled cookie sheet with point under. Brush generously with oil, let rise until very light and bake at 350° for about 20 minutes until toast-brown and crisp. These are delicious hot, cold or reheated.

FOR SPECIAL DIETS:
—sugar may be replaced by equivalent amount of sweetener.

SUBSTITUTIONS WHICH MAY BE MADE:
—Instant Beef Bouillon and water may be used in place of canned consommé when reconstituted according to directions on container.
—butter or margarine may be used in place of butter-flavored oil.
—paper-thin slices of baked ham or Canadian bacon may be used instead of dried beef.

SPECIAL EVERYDAY BREAD

1 package dry yeast
½ teaspoon sugar
¼ teaspoon ginger
¼ cup warm water
2 cups warm water
½ cup instant dried whey
¼ cup honey

⅓ cup each gluten, corn, potato and graham flours, rice polish and quick hominy grits
¼ cup vegetable shortening, softened
1½ teaspoons salt
½ cup bran buds
3 cups white flour

(Measure and combine the six ⅓ cup portions of flours,

polish and grits before starting to make dough so that yeast will not have to stand too long.)

Put yeast, sugar and ginger in small bowl. Pour in ¼ cup warm water and stir well. Set in warm place until foaming. In large bowl mix together 2 cups warm water, ½ cup whey, honey and the 2 cups combined gluten, corn, potato, graham flours and rice polish and hominy grits. Mix well. Add the foaming yeast and beat until smooth. Add the soft vegetable shortening, salt, bran buds and 2 cups white flour. Stir until well mixed. Spread the remaining 1 cup white flour on the pastry board. Turn out dough and knead thoroughly, working in a little more flour if necessary to make a good stiff dough (if after baking the loaves flatten a little in center, the dough has not been quite stiff enough). Divide in halves, shape into loaves and place in well greased 8½x3½x 2½-inch pans. Brush tops generously with shortening or butter, cover and let set in warm place until dough has rounded up slightly above rim of pans (this will take a little longer than an all-white flour dough). Bake in oven preheated to 350° for 40 to 45 minutes. If crust is becoming browner than desired, reduce temperature for last 15 minutes of baking period.

This makes 2 high, light loaves with a very distinctive, rich, "country flavor" which older people will remember with fondness.

FOR SPECIAL DIETS:
—salt may be omitted or salt substitute used in equivalent amount.

SUBSTITUTIONS WHICH MAY BE MADE:
—honey may be replaced by equal amount of sorghum.
—dried whey may be replaced by equal amount of powdered buttermilk.
—vegetable shortening may be replaced by butter or margarine in equal amount.

(The list of ingredients in this bread follow as nearly as is possible for this home baker, that which is printed on the wrapper of a "country style" bread widely distributed in this area by a commercial baker which is delicious but very apt to be badly mashed in its loose plastic wrapper before the grocery shopper gets it home.)

SUNFLOWER HONEY BREAD

1 package dry yeast	1 cup white flour
½ teaspoon sugar	3 eggs, beaten
¼ teaspoon ginger	¼ cup margarine, softened
¼ cup warm water	1 teaspoon salt
1½ cups buttermilk	1 teaspoon mace, optional
4 tablespoons honey	2 teaspoons strawberry
1 cup sunflower seed meal	flavoring, optional
1 cup rolled wheat	3 cups white flour

Put yeast, sugar and ginger in small bowl. Pour in warm water and stir well. Set in warm place until foaming. Heat buttermilk until comfortably warm. In large bowl mix together the buttermilk, honey, sunflower meal, rolled wheat and 1 cup white flour. Add foaming yeast and beat well. Add beaten eggs, margarine, salt, mace and strawberry flavoring (neither the mace nor flavoring are necessary but they do help to eliminate the rather raw, acrid taste which some sunflower meal has), and 2 cups white flour. Mix well. Spread remaining 1 cup white flour on the pastry board. Turn out dough and knead thoroughly working in a little more flour if necessary to make a good stiff dough. Divide in halves, shape into loaves and place in well-greased 8½x 3½x2½-inch pans. Brush tops with margarine, cover and let set in warm place until tops of loaves round up above rim of pan. Bake in oven preheated to 350° 40 to 45 minutes. After first 15 minutes, reduce heat to 325° for remainder of baking period. This recipe makes 2 loaves. This makes a very light, moist bread. Toasted it is delicious with practically everything from breakfast coffee to a light supper of toast, milk and fruit.

FOR SPECIAL DIETS:

—salt may be omitted or equivalent amount of substitute used.

SUBSTITUTIONS WHICH MAY BE USED:

—1½ cups warm water and 9 tablespoons powdered butter-milk may replace the cultured buttermilk.

—margarine may be replaced with equal amount of butter or butter-flavored oil.

—mace may be omitted or replaced by equal amount of all-spice.

—strawberry flavoring may be omitted or replaced by any other favorite such as lemon, banana, apricot brandy, etc.

THRIFTY FRUIT BREAD

1 package dry yeast	2 cups flour
½ teaspoon sugar	½ cup dry skim milk
¼ teaspoon ginger	3 whole eggs or 6 yolks plus
¼ cup warm water	2 tablespoons water
1½ cups canned sweetened peach juice	¼ cup butter-flavored oil
	1½ teaspoons salt
1 to 2 teaspoons fruit brandy essence (optional)	3½ cups flour

Put yeast, sugar and ginger in small bowl. Pour in warm water and stir thoroughly. Set in warm place until foaming. Heat peach juice to just comfortably warm. In large bowl mix it with the brandy essence, 2 cups flour and dried milk. Add the foaming yeast and beat well. Add beaten eggs, oil, salt and 2½ cups flour. Stir until dough is well mixed. Spread remaining 1 cup flour on pastry board. Turn out dough and knead thoroughly. Divide in halves, shape into loaves and place in well-oiled 8½x3½x2½-inch pans. Brush tops generously with oil or butter, cover and set in warm place until dough has rounded up above rim of pans. Bake in oven preheated to 350°, 45 minutes for loaves, 25 to 30 minutes for rolls or coffee cake. This recipe will make 2 large loaves. It is nice to make 1 loaf, 1 crumb-topped coffee cake in 12x4-

inch roll pan, and 8 to 12 rolls of the Belgian Cramique type. Work ½ cup of currants and ½ teaspoon anise seed into a half-loaf portion of dough. Divide into equal portion for number of rolls desired, whether tiny or medium size. Divide each little portion into pieces about ¾ to ¼ proportion. Make the larger into balls and place in round layer cake pan. Make each of the smaller pieces into teardrop shape, slit tops of large balls and push each pointed end well down into slit. Brush generously with melted butter, cover and let rise until very light. Bake as directed above. If a sweet roll is desired, when baked and cooled, dribble a rich almond or rum-flavored icing over tops. These rolls quite often disappear before mealtime unless hidden!

FOR SPECIAL DIETS:
—salt may be omitted.
—unsweetened juice may be used and an amount of sweetener equal to ½ cup sugar added.

SUBSTITUTIONS WHICH MAY BE MADE:

—any other canned juice such as plum, pineapple, cherry, etc. This is a good way to use up surplus juice when making fancy desserts using only the drained fruit.

—using egg yolks in place of whole eggs is economical; use those left after making meringues, sponge cakes, etc.

—butter or margarine may be used in place of the oil in equal amount.

THRIFTY VEGETABLE BREAD

1 package dry yeast	2 tablespoons sugar
½ teaspoon sugar	½ cup dry potato buds
¼ teaspoon ginger	2 cups white flour
¼ cup warm water	¼ cup butter-flavored oil
1½ cups liquid from canned green beans	1½ teaspoons salt
½ cup V-8 or tomato juice	3 cups white flour

Put yeast, sugar and ginger in small bowl. Pour in warm water and stir well. Set in warm place until foaming. Heat green bean liquid and V-8 or tomato juice until just comfortably warm. In a large bowl mix the juices with sugar, potato buds and 2 cups white flour. Stir in the foaming yeast. Add oil, salt and 2 cups white flour. Mix well. Spread remaining 1 cup flour on pastry board. Turn out dough and knead thoroughly. Divide in halves. Shape into loaves and place in well oiled 8½x3½x2½-inch pans. Brush tops with oil or butter, cover and set in warm place until dough rounds up just above rim of pans. Bake in oven preheated to 350° for 40 to 45 minutes depending on how brown a crust is desired. (This bread has such a delicate fluffy texture, crisp crust and appetizing flavor it is a perfect accompaniment to almost any main dish or salad. It is also especially good for meat sandwiches and so it is nice to make up half or all of the dough into hamburger buns and weiner rolls to store in freezer.)

FOR SPECIAL DIETS:
—salt may be omitted or replaced by equivalent in substitute.
—sugar may be replaced by equivalent amount of sweetener.

SUBSTITUTIONS WHICH MAY BE MADE:
—liquids from other canned vegetables such as corn, hominy, dried beans, etc., or combination of any, may be used and for salt-free diets only those from unseasoned products should be used.
—any softened shortening preferred may replace the oil in the same amount.

TOASTED OATMEAL BREAD

2 cups quick oatmeal, toasted
1 package dry yeast
½ teaspoon sugar
¼ teaspoon ginger
¼ cup warm water
1½ cups warm water
½ cup dry coffee creamer
½ cup brown-sugar
½ teaspoon maple flavoring
1 teaspoon salt
¼ cup margarine, softened
1 cup grated salted peanuts
2 eggs beaten
4 cups white flour

(Prepare quick oatmeal before starting to mix dough. Spread the 2 cups quick oatmeal on cookie sheet and toast to a light brown in oven, watching carefully and stirring often to prevent it from becoming too brown in places.)

Put yeast, sugar and ginger in small bowl. Pour in ¼ cup warm water and stir well. Set in warm place until foaming. In large bowl mix together 1½ cups warm water, coffee creamer, brown sugar and the toasted oatmeal. Add foaming yeast and beat well. Add maple flavoring, salt, soft margarine, grated peanuts (if using small ones, remove skins), beaten eggs and 3 cups white flour. Stir until well mixed. Spread remaining 1 cup white flour on pastry board. Turn out dough and knead thoroughly, using a little more flour if necessary to make a very stiff dough. Divide in halves, shape into loaves and place in well-greased 8½x3½x 2½-inch pans. Brush tops generously with margarine, cover and let set in warm place until dough rounds up slightly above rim of pans (if it becomes too light it will sink a little in center of loaf while baking). Bake in oven preheated to 375° for 40 to 45 minutes. After 20 minutes reduce temperature to 350 for remainder of baking period. This recipe makes 2 high, light, crisp-crusted loaves of bread which is an all time family favorite for eating with grape jelly. It is not recommended for adjusting to special diets.

SUBSTITUTIONS WHICH MAY BE MADE:

—½ cup vanilla-flavored Instant Breakfast mix may be used in place of coffee creamer.

—caramel or butterscotch may be used in place of maple flavoring.

—butter or butter-flavored oil may be used in place of margarine.

—salted cashew nuts may be used in place of peanuts.

TRIPLE CORN BREAD

1 package dry yeast	1½ cups yellow cornmeal
½ teaspoon sugar	1 cup white flour
¼ teaspoon ginger	½ cup powdered buttermilk
¼ cup warm water	3 eggs, well beaten
*1½ cups liquid from whole canned sweet corn	¼ cup corn oil margarine
	1½ teaspoons seasoned salt
¼ cup sugar	3½ cups white flour

Put yeast, sugar and ginger in small bowl. Pour in warm water and stir well. Set in warm place until foaming. Heat corn liquid until comfortably warm. Pour into large bowl and mix well with the ¼ cup sugar, 1½ cups corn meal, 1 cup white flour and ½ cup powdered buttermilk. Add foaming yeast and beat well. Add eggs, softened margarine, seasoned salt and 2½ cups white flour. Mix until dough clears the bowl. Spread remaining 1 cup flour on the pastry board. Turn out dough and knead thoroughly using a little more flour if necessary to make a good stiff dough. Divide in halves, shape into loaves and place in well greased 8½x3½x 2½-inch pans. Brush tops with margarine, cover and set in warm place to raise until dough is even with rim of pans. Bake in oven preheated to 350° for 40 to 45 minutes. After 15 minutes, when crust has just begun to brown, reduce temperature to 325° for remainder of baking period. This recipe makes 2 loaves. The bread has a very even, fine texture and is delicious with any well seasoned meat or vegetable dishes.

* This amount of liquid can usually be obtained from 2 No. 303 cans of "family style" corn. If there is not quite enough, complete the measure with water. This is a good way to use up the liquid usually discarded when making corn soufflé and other similar dishes. The liquid can be kept for several days in refrigerator before using or the bread can be made up at once as it freezes very well.

FOR SPECIAL DIETS:
—salt may be omitted or replaced by equivalent amount of substitute but the bread will not have quite the same zesty flavor.
—sugar may be replaced by equivalent amount of artificial sweetener.

SUBSTITUTIONS WHICH MAY BE MADE:
—white corn meal may be used in place of the yellow but bread will not have as attractive a color.
—corn syrup may replace sugar, making it a quadruple corn bread.
—powdered buttermilk may be replaced by same amount of dry skim milk.

WHITE RICE BREAD

1 package dry yeast
½ teaspoon sugar
¼ teaspoon ginger
¼ cup warm water
1½ cups warm water
1 cup cream of rice soup
1 envelope (2 oz.) dry
  topping mix powder

½ cup white corn syrup
2 cups white flour
¼ cup margarine, softened
1½ teaspoons salt
3 cups white flour

Put yeast, sugar and ginger in small bowl. Pour in ¼ cup warm water and stir well. Set in warm place until foaming. In large bowl mix together 1½ cups warm water, cream of rice, topping mix powder, corn syrup and 2 cups white flour. Add the foaming yeast and beat well. Add soft margarine, salt and 2 cups white flour. Mix well. Spread remaining 1 cup white flour on the pastry board. Turn out dough and knead well, working in as much flour as necessary to make a fairly stiff dough. Divide in halves, shape into loaves and place in well greased 8½x3½x2½-inch pans. Brush tops generously with margarine, cover and set in warm place until dough rounds up a little above rim of pans. Bake in oven preheated to 350° for 40 to 45 minutes. This recipe will make 2 loaves with such excellent flavor and texture it can be used for all general purposes, and is especially good for making croutons to use in main-dish vegetable salads or to float in bowls of hot soups.

To prepare croutons: cut bread into ½-inch slices, then into ½-inch cubes. Toss lightly in melted butter or margarine and spread out on flat pan to toast quickly under broiler.

FOR SPECIAL DIETS:
—salt may be omitted or equivalent amount of substitute used.

SUBSTITUTIONS WHICH MAY BE MADE:
—butter, butter-flavored oil may replace the margarine.

RUSKS

Use recipe for Canadian Rusks (page 24) following directions for shaping. Omit the coating of sugar and spice if desired. If left plain, cover with sheet of plastic wrapping or very thin damp cloth while raising. Round rusks may also be made by rolling dough to about ½-inch thickness. Place on greased cookie sheet far enough apart so as not to touch when light. Cover as above until ready for oven. Bake in oven preheated to 375° for about 20 minutes until lightly browned. Brush with hot water or a mixture of 1 teaspoon of milk to 1 tablespoon sugar. When completely cooled, split each bun in two and place halves on cookie sheets and dry out in oven as directed. (Flavor of Rusks may be varied by adding to the dough 1 cup currants or ½ to ¾ cup grated orange peel or 2 teaspoons very finely crushed fennel.)

RAISING MONEY WITH BREAD

It has been my experience that nothing commands a better price or is more easily sold at bazaars and other fund-raising events than bread. I don't recall ever having helped with or visited one of these sales where the breads weren't the very first items to be completely sold out. As far as I know the most paid for a loaf of my bread was $4.25 at a Junior League sale to raise funds for their work in the city hospitals. It was

Polish Babka baked in a bundt pan. I donated forty-six loaves which sold for a total of $96.

"Order and Deliver" sale

One church organization in a large city has a spring and fall "Order and Deliver" sale of baked foods. A lady who is a member gave these details of the project. The women are divided into three groups. Those who like to bake volunteer to produce a certain number of loaves (or other forms) of their favorite bread or other baked foods. The second group has charge of making up the order sheets and taking the customer's orders. The third serve as drivers to deliver the food on a certain date. This has proved so successful for a number of years that, even before the order lists are made up, there are usually more requests (especially for the most popular breads) than can be filled. This is such a good plan for it allows all the members of the women's organization to take an active part in the project, even those who are unable to stay away from home long enough to help with an all-day food sale, the woman who is in a wheelchair or even bedfast can use the telephone to take orders and those who can drive do their share in delivering.

"Pay-As-You-Taste"

Here, in Miami County, Kansas, for the fund-raising project of our County Extension Homemakers Council there is a "Penny-A-Taste" table (it could be a Nickel- or a Dime-A-Taste) at the annual Hobby Lobby Day each year. This is a very practical idea where the activities are held in an auditorium with no kitchen facilities. Members of the various units are asked to donate breads and other baked foods (which can be eaten with fingers only). Then the only items which have to be purchased are covering for the table, small paper pie plates, and paper cups for free coffee. Each person who is to do the baking is asked to send in the recipe she will use at least a month before the event. Copies of these are made into little booklets and one of the Units designs and makes attractive covers for them. They are sold for 25 cents each. (Again, you could charge more: 50 cents, perhaps, where printing costs may run higher than they do here.)

The breads and all other foods are cut into finger-size portions preferably before bringing them to the hall. Each "taster" goes the length of the table, loading her plate with goodies, deposits the change in the box, picks up a free cup of coffee and finds a place to sit, rest and nibble before going to the next exhibit or craft lesson. Many make the trip back to the table several times during the day and each taster always checks in the booklet she has also purchased to make sure which recipe goes with which things she particularly liked.

Each year more food is brought in and more booklets printed but always the table is cleared of both before the last visitors arrive and they are really disappointed. Last year, for the first time, a small table of only diet breads and other foods was added and it was a great success. There are a lot of penny-sized portions in a large loaf of bread and the coins soon fill the box.

I am sure that a "Taste" table would be well worth the effort in connection with any all-day food sale such as many organizations hold from time to time in the best location to be secured in a downtown store, especially if the table could be set up in a show window to tempt people to come inside. Of course, bread is the easiest food to cut into finger-size portions and display attractively.

Plant sales and house-and-garden tours

An experienced helper in raising funds says that it is a known fact that people attending these functions stay longer, enjoy themselves more and buy more if there is food and drink available. Many organizations have spring house-and-garden tours or plant sales not only for members but the public as well. At a home where there is a lovely garden or a convenient space, either outdoors or in, for serving food, it adds greatly to the success of the sale to have a refreshment table. Since these are usually held in the morning, a variety of fancy breads and coffee are most suitable; for an afternoon tour, a tea table should be featured. The refreshments can either be free or a box with a tactful notice about a donation to whatever cause the money is being raised for may be placed on the table. Of course, small rolls, tiny muffins, etc., are most attractive and easiest to handle but many will appreciate sliced breads too with jelly or preserves and butter.

Breads around the world

Study and Travel clubs often have teas, luncheons, or dinners to raise funds for paying their guest speakers or for renting film or slides for programs. If they have been concentrating on one certain country at the time, then at least one dish of that country should be featured. A good way to get information on foods, decorations, etc. is to contact the Information Department of that country's embassy in Washington, D. C. They can usually be helpful with such things as recipe leaflets, posters, and suggestions.

Here are a few sample suggestions of foods from various countries (all using bread, of course) which are easy to prepare. With the many good cookbooks published on foreign foods, detailed recipes are easily obtained.

FROM POLAND
—Apple Soup
—Croutons: Use a plain white bread, butter the slices on both sides, stack and cut into cubes. Toast quickly in 450° oven and be sure to make a good supply.
—Hot Coffee or Chocolate (in winter)
—Iced Beverage (in summer)

FROM FINLAND
—Cold Fruit Soup
—Finnish Vipuri Twists or Freshly Crisped Rusks (see index for recipes)

FROM AUSTRIA
—Salad Luncheon
—Cottage Cheese Spread: Cream 1 pound small curd and fairly dry cottage cheese with 4 tablespoons butter. Season to taste with salt, pepper and about 1 teaspoon sweet red paprika (just enough to give cheese a light pinkish tint). Add 2 tablespoons each of chives, finely chopped, and caraway seed and 3 tablespoons beer. Mix well and chill thoroughly. Can be served in thin slices if desired.
—Plenty of Thin Toasted Triangles of White and Rye Bread

FROM RUSSIA
—Russian Brown Betty: Use rye bread crumbs which have no seeds (Really Rye Bread is good for this); serve hot or cold with whipped topping. An especially good dessert for winter affairs.
   Peel and core 4 large tart apples (Winesap or Jonathan preferred). Cut into eighths and simmer in covered saucepan with ½ cup water, ½ cup sugar and ½ to 1 cup golden raisins until tender. Stir in 1 teaspoon grated orange rind. Sauté 3 cups finely crumbled fresh rye bread in 2 tablespoons butter just until they start to brown. Stir in ½ cup sugar and ½ teaspoon cloves. Butter a medium-size glass loaf pan or casserole. Dust bottom and sides with fine dry bread crumbs or coconut meal. Put in ⅓ of the sautéed bread crumbs and pat into an even layer. Spoon the apples and raisins over this layer. Sprinkle top of fruit with 1

teaspoon cinnamon. Add a second layer of crumbs and spread the preserves over this. Top with remaining crumbs. Cover pan with aluminum foil and bake in oven preheated to 325° for 1 hour. Remove foil and turn heat up for just a few minutes until top is crisp and crunchy.

FROM DENMARK

For a Morning Coffee or "Come as You Are" Breakfast
—Danish Rum Rolls (see index for recipe)
—Hot Coffee

FROM U.S.A.

From our own beautiful country plan menus around the Pennsylvania Dutch, Shakers, and others.
—Pennsylvania Dutch—Use dough from Thumb Print Coffee Cake (page 88) to make *Kartoffel Twists*, large, long loaves of double braids. Divide loaf size portion of dough into about ⅔ and ⅓ portions. Make three-strand braids of each. Place larger braid in well-greased loaf pan. Brush top with milk and place smaller braid on top. Brush top generously with butter and let set in warm place until light. Bake in 350° oven about 45 to 50 minutes, until crust is beautifully brown.
—Shakers—Perfect White Bread (page 19) and Latin Brown Bread can be used to make the white and graham bread in single large, square loaves or narrow, high loaves baked three or four together in large flat pans such as we call sheet-cake pans today (I remember seeing some old, old ones of beautiful speckled blue granite).
—Creole—serve Savarin Bread (page 56) with pitchers of hot, clear raspberry, apricot and rum syrups to be used as toppings. (These can be bought in most gourmet shops.) Include Frosty Whipped Cream set in a bowl of crushed ice, and mounds of chopped nuts, toasted coconut and diced candied fruit to be sprinkled over the syrups. Add a beverage, of course.

LETTERS, LETTERS, LETTERS

One of the nicest results of having a cookbook published is the letters the author receives from so many interested and interesting people. (A few have been critical, but that too is good. It keeps one from becoming complacent.) I was pleased that so many people enjoyed my recipes enough that they wanted to share their favorites with me. There have been some from dear old ladies whose writing was so shaky it could barely be deciphered and many from young servicemen's wives, returning home from overseas tours of duty, where they became acquainted with homemade bread for the first time. Best of all was the fact that my first book was the key to a lovely friendship with a famous author whose work I had admired for many years.

Sometime ago, when I was asked to give a short talk at a cooking contest, it was suggested that I tell about some of the most unusual letters I had received. I had to do this mostly from memory. I had started to keep a file of letters but, before long, it soon became apparent that if I did, after awhile there would be no room for anything else so they all had to go.

One woman wrote that the only reason she bought the book was because of the jacket design which was just like the print in a dress she had had while still living in England and it made her homesick. Then, after she looked through it she knew she had to start learning to bake bread, a thing she had never done before and she was having great fun. She hoped I was a fellow countrywoman and we could get acquainted.

A Pennsylvania gentleman of some 80 years who, from his name might have been a distant relative, wrote several times. He was having trouble making the bread with starter and,

he did so want to make it right for he remembered how good
it tasted when his wife was alive to make it for him. I helped
him as much as I could with suggestions. The last letter
notified me that he would not have to bother me anymore
as the bread was now turning out alright. He had been given
a new heating pad for his lame knee so he could now use
the old one to keep the starter at the right temperature overnight!

An Oklahoma woman wanted to know if there was a mis-
print in a certain recipe because it took almost twice as much
flour to make a workable dough and she thought someone
had done a poor job of proofreading. Before I had time to
reply, I received another letter which had been posted the
day after the first one, containing an apology. As soon as she
had mailed it she remembered that she had been called to
the door during the mixing and when she returned to the
kitchen she had absent-mindedly added a second measure of
liquid. She concluded that the bread turned out fine though,
and she would continue to make it that way for her large
family.

A prominent doctor from an Eastern city let me know that,
because he enjoyed baking so much for relaxation, he was
advising his men patients (who were in a position to do so)
to also take it up as a hobby. If knitting was good therapy
he was sure bread making was even better, and he was advising all to use my book as a beginner's text.

A Jewish gentleman from the Midwest wrote for permis-
sion to give some of my recipes in an article to be published
about his breads which had won prizes at a County Fair.
Later, he also sent a copy of the article with pictures of
some of the entries and also one of him at work. I was very
proud of him.

A woman living at an Army base in Germany had been given a copy of my book and all the other wives in the living quarters who had shared her breads wanted copies so she was asking the PX to stock it in their book department if possible.

Another letter from the wife of an Air Force Major who had been stationed on the other side of the world told of becoming interested in baking because the family missed bread so much; she had even helped to establish a small home bakery near their post. After she returned to the States she continued baking regularly, always making enough each time to share with some other family at their station.

This is just a small sampling of the letters I have enjoyed through the years which have made me happy. The majority of them have been lovely "sharing" letters from many states and overseas—from England, Holland, Germany, Finland, France and even as far away as Australia.

FREEZING AND REHEATING BREADS

It is very disappointing that the fine cellophane wrap which was so perfect for storing bread is no longer being sold. With its many drawbacks, the plastic wrap is the best to use now. While hard to handle, it makes much neater and tighter packages than can be made with aluminum foil and resists punctures better. The bread must then be rewrapped in foil or wax paper before being reheated. The wax paper is to be preferred because of its transparency—one can check the condition of the bread while in the oven so as not to let it become too moist or too brown.

Any bread can be stored in the freezer when well sealed for indefinite periods of time and many breads rich with nuts or fruits or spices or combinations of these gain flavor from being stored. All bread should be wrapped as soon as cool to avoid loss of moisture. Preslicing all loaves (except any which are needed whole for some special purpose) is a great time-saver when they are to be used. If only a part of a loaf is needed, the slices can be easily pried apart with knife while still frozen and a few slices reheated much quicker and at a higher temperature than a whole loaf.

Rolls and coffee cakes containing fillings may do better to be completely thawed and then reheated quickly at a higher temperature without any wrapping if they are very moist.

Dry-type breads such as those containing several eggs (Egg Pastry, Babka, etc.), ground meals (Triple Corn Bread, Cocoanut Custard Bread) and dry cereals (Toasted Oatmeal Bread) are best partially thawed and then reheated at low temperature still sealed.

Breads with more moisture-retaining ingredients such as mashed potatoes (All Rye Bread) should be completely thawed and then reheated in partially open wrapper.

Hard-crusted breads (Beer Bread) will have softened crusts unless completely thawed and then reheated with openings at both ends of wrapper. The best way of all if this type bread is to be used at once is to pry frozen slices apart, spread with butter and heat quickly on baking sheet under broiler.

Rich and moist loaves (Date Pudding Bread, Pineapple Yogurt Bread) should be completely thawed before reheating at very low temperature with wrapper partially open. With any of the breads, if the wrapper becomes very steamy during reheating, puncture it in several places with point of knife.

INDEX

A CATALOGUE OF
SELECTED DOVER BOOKS
IN ALL FIELDS OF INTEREST

A CATALOGUE OF SELECTED DOVER BOOKS IN ALL FIELDS OF INTEREST

CELESTIAL OBJECTS FOR COMMON TELESCOPES, T. W. Webb. The most used book in amateur astronomy: inestimable aid for locating and identifying nearly 4,000 celestial objects. Edited, updated by Margaret W. Mayall. 77 illustrations. Total of 645pp. 5⅜ x 8½.
20917-2, 20918-0 Pa., Two-vol. set $9.00

HISTORICAL STUDIES IN THE LANGUAGE OF CHEMISTRY, M. P. Crosland. The important part language has played in the development of chemistry from the symbolism of alchemy to the adoption of systematic nomenclature in 1892. ". . . wholeheartedly recommended,"—Science. 15 illustrations. 416pp. of text. 5⅝ x 8¼. 63702-6 Pa. $6.00

BURNHAM'S CELESTIAL HANDBOOK, Robert Burnham, Jr. Thorough, readable guide to the stars beyond our solar system. Exhaustive treatment, fully illustrated. Breakdown is alphabetical by constellation: Andromeda to Cetus in Vol. 1; Chamaeleon to Orion in Vol. 2; and Pavo to Vulpecula in Vol. 3. Hundreds of illustrations. Total of about 2000pp. 6⅛ x 9¼.
23567-X, 23568-8, 23673-0 Pa., Three-vol. set $26.85

THEORY OF WING SECTIONS: INCLUDING A SUMMARY OF AIRFOIL DATA, Ira H. Abbott and A. E. von Doenhoff. Concise compilation of subatomic aerodynamic characteristics of modern NASA wing sections, plus description of theory. 350pp. of tables. 693pp. 5⅜ x 8½.
60586-8 Pa. $7.00

DE RE METALLICA, Georgius Agricola. Translated by Herbert C. Hoover and Lou H. Hoover. The famous Hoover translation of greatest treatise on technological chemistry, engineering, geology, mining of early modern times (1556). All 289 original woodcuts. 638pp. 6¾ x 11.
60006-8 Clothbd. $17.50

THE ORIGIN OF CONTINENTS AND OCEANS, Alfred Wegener. One of the most influential, most controversial books in science, the classic statement for continental drift. Full 1966 translation of Wegener's final (1929) version. 64 illustrations. 246pp. 5⅜ x 8½. 61708-4 Pa. $3.00

THE PRINCIPLES OF PSYCHOLOGY, William James. Famous long course complete, unabridged. Stream of thought, time perception, memory, experimental methods; great work decades ahead of its time. Still valid, useful; read in many classes. 94 figures. Total of 1391pp. 5⅜ x 8½.
20381-6, 20382-4 Pa., Two-vol. set $13.00

YUCATAN BEFORE AND AFTER THE CONQUEST, Diego de Landa. First English translation of basic book in Maya studies, the only significant account of Yucatan written in the early post-Conquest era. Translated by distinguished Maya scholar William Gates. Appendices, introduction, 4 maps and over 120 illustrations added by translator. 162pp. 5⅜ x 8½.
23622-6 Pa. $3.00

THE MALAY ARCHIPELAGO, Alfred R. Wallace. Spirited travel account by one of founders of modern biology. Touches on zoology, botany, ethnography, geography, and geology. 62 illustrations, maps. 515pp. 5⅜ x 8½.
20187-2 Pa. $6.95

THE DISCOVERY OF THE TOMB OF TUTANKHAMEN, Howard Carter, A. C. Mace. Accompany Carter in the thrill of discovery, as ruined passage suddenly reveals unique, untouched, fabulously rich tomb. Fascinating account, with 106 illustrations. New introduction by J. M. White. Total of 382pp. 5⅜ x 8½. (Available in U.S. only) 23500-9 Pa. $4.00

THE WORLD'S GREATEST SPEECHES, edited by Lewis Copeland and Lawrence W. Lamm. Vast collection of 278 speeches from Greeks up to present. Powerful and effective models; unique look at history. Revised to 1970. Indices. 842pp. 5⅜ x 8½.
20468-5 Pa. $8.95

THE 100 GREATEST ADVERTISEMENTS, Julian Watkins. The priceless ingredient; His master's voice; 99 44/100% pure; over 100 others. How they were written, their impact, etc. Remarkable record. 130 illustrations. 233pp. 7⅞ x 10 3/5.
20540-1 Pa. $5.00

CRUICKSHANK PRINTS FOR HAND COLORING, George Cruickshank. 18 illustrations, one side of a page, on fine-quality paper suitable for watercolors. Caricatures of people in society (c. 1820) full of trenchant wit. Very large format. 32pp. 11 x 16.
23684-6 Pa. $5.00

THIRTY-TWO COLOR POSTCARDS OF TWENTIETH-CENTURY AMERICAN ART, Whitney Museum of American Art. Reproduced in full color in postcard form are 31 art works and one shot of the museum. Calder, Hopper, Rauschenberg, others. Detachable. 16pp. 8¼ x 11.
23629-3 Pa. $2.50

MUSIC OF THE SPHERES: THE MATERIAL UNIVERSE FROM ATOM TO QUASAR SIMPLY EXPLAINED, Guy Murchie. Planets, stars, geology, atoms, radiation, relativity, quantum theory, light, antimatter, similar topics. 319 figures. 664pp. 5⅜ x 8½.
21809-0, 21810-4 Pa., Two-vol. set $10.00

EINSTEIN'S THEORY OF RELATIVITY, Max Born. Finest semi-technical account; covers Einstein, Lorentz, Minkowski, and others, with much detail, much explanation of ideas and math not readily available elsewhere on this level. For student, non-specialist. 376pp. 5⅜ x 8½.
60769-0 Pa. $4.00

THE COMPLETE BOOK OF DOLL MAKING AND COLLECTING, Catherine Christopher. Instructions, patterns for dozens of dolls, from rag doll on up to elaborate, historically accurate figures. Mould faces, sew clothing, make doll houses, etc. Also collecting information. Many illustrations. 288pp. 6 x 9.　　　　　　　　　　　　　22066-4 Pa. $4.00

THE DAGUERREOTYPE IN AMERICA, Beaumont Newhall. Wonderful portraits, 1850's townscapes, landscapes; full text plus 104 photographs. The basic book. Enlarged 1976 edition. 272pp. 8¼ x 11¼.
23322-7 Pa. $6.00

CRAFTSMAN HOMES, Gustav Stickley. 296 architectural drawings, floor plans, and photographs illustrate 40 different kinds of "Mission-style" homes from *The Craftsman* (1901-16), voice of American style of simplicity and organic harmony. Thorough coverage of Craftsman idea in text and picture, now collector's item. 224pp. 8⅛ x 11.　　　23791-5 Pa. $6.00

PEWTER-WORKING: INSTRUCTIONS AND PROJECTS, Burl N. Osborn. & Gordon O. Wilber. Introduction to pewter-working for amateur craftsman. History and characteristics of pewter; tools, materials, step-by-step instructions. Photos, line drawings, diagrams. Total of 160pp. 7⅞ x 10¾.　　　　　　　　　　　　　23786-9 Pa. $3.50

THE GREAT CHICAGO FIRE, edited by David Lowe. 10 dramatic, eyewitness accounts of the 1871 disaster, including one of the aftermath and rebuilding, plus 70 contemporary photographs and illustrations of the ruins—courthouse, Palmer House, Great Central Depot, etc. Introduction by David Lowe. 87pp. 8¼ x 11.　　　　　　　　23771-0 Pa. $4.00

SILHOUETTES: A PICTORIAL ARCHIVE OF VARIED ILLUSTRATIONS, edited by Carol Belanger Grafton. Over 600 silhouettes from the 18th to 20th centuries include profiles and full figures of men and women, children, birds and animals, groups and scenes, nature, ships, an alphabet. Dozens of uses for commercial artists and craftspeople. 144pp. 8⅜ x 11¼.
23781-8 Pa. $4.00

ANIMALS: 1,419 COPYRIGHT-FREE ILLUSTRATIONS OF MAMMALS, BIRDS, FISH, INSECTS, ETC., edited by Jim Harter. Clear wood engravings present, in extremely lifelike poses, over 1,000 species of animals. One of the most extensive copyright-free pictorial sourcebooks of its kind. Captions. Index. 284pp. 9 x 12.　　　　　　23766-4 Pa. $7.50

INDIAN DESIGNS FROM ANCIENT ECUADOR, Frederick W. Shaffer. 282 original designs by pre-Columbian Indians of Ecuador (500-1500 A.D.). Designs include people, mammals, birds, reptiles, fish, plants, heads, geometric designs. Use as is or alter for advertising, textiles, leathercraft, etc. Introduction. 95pp. 8¾ x 11¼.　　　　　　　　23764-8 Pa. $3.50

SZIGETI ON THE VIOLIN, Joseph Szigeti. Genial, loosely structured tour by premier violinist, featuring a pleasant mixture of reminiscenes, insights into great music and musicians, innumerable tips for practicing violinists. 385 musical passages. 256pp. 5⅝ x 8¼.　　　23763-X Pa. $3.50

TONE POEMS, SERIES II: TILL EULENSPIEGELS LUSTIGE STREICHE, ALSO SPRACH ZARATHUSTRA, AND EIN HELDEN-LEBEN, Richard Strauss. Three important orchestral works, including very popular *Till Eulenspiegel's Marry Pranks*, reproduced in full score from original editions. Study score. 315pp. 9⅜ x 12¼. (Available in U.S. only)
23755-9 Pa. $7.50

TONE POEMS, SERIES I: DON JUAN, TOD UND VERKLARUNG AND DON QUIXOTE, Richard Strauss. Three of the most often performed and recorded works in entire orchestral repertoire, reproduced in full score from original editions. Study score. 286pp. 9⅜ x 12¼. (Available in U.S. only)
23754-0 Pa. $7.50

11 LATE STRING QUARTETS, Franz Joseph Haydn. The form which Haydn defined and "brought to perfection." (*Grove's*). 11 string quartets in complete score, his last and his best. The first in a projected series of the complete Haydn string quartets. Reliable modern Eulenberg edition, otherwise difficult to obtain. 320pp. 8⅜ x 11¼. (Available in U.S. only)
23753-2 Pa. $6.95

FOURTH, FIFTH AND SIXTH SYMPHONIES IN FULL SCORE, Peter Ilyitch Tchaikovsky. Complete orchestral scores of Symphony No. 4 in F Minor, Op. 36; Symphony No. 5 in E Minor, Op. 64; Symphony No. 6 in B Minor, "Pathetique," Op. 74. Bretikopf & Hartel eds. Study score. 480pp. 9⅜ x 12¼.
23861-X Pa. $10.95

THE MARRIAGE OF FIGARO: COMPLETE SCORE, Wolfgang A. Mozart. Finest comic opera ever written. Full score, not to be confused with piano renderings. Peters edition. Study score. 448pp. 9⅜ x 12¼. (Available in U.S. only)
23751-6 Pa. $11.95

"IMAGE" ON THE ART AND EVOLUTION OF THE FILM, edited by Marshall Deutelbaum. Pioneering book brings together for first time 38 groundbreaking articles on early silent films from *Image* and 263 illustrations newly shot from rare prints in the collection of the International Museum of Photography. A landmark work. Index. 256pp. 8¼ x 11.
23777-X Pa. $8.95

AROUND-THE-WORLD COOKY BOOK, Lois Lintner Sumption and Marguerite Lintner Ashbrook. 373 cooky and frosting recipes from 28 countries (America, Austria, China, Russia, Italy, etc.) include Viennese kisses, rice wafers, London strips, lady fingers, hony, sugar spice, maple cookies, etc. Clear instructions. All tested. 38 drawings. 182pp. 5⅜ x 8.
23802-4 Pa. $2.50

THE ART NOUVEAU STYLE, edited by Roberta Waddell. 579 rare photographs, not available elsewhere, of works in jewelry, metalwork, glass, ceramics, textiles, architecture and furniture by 175 artists—Mucha, Seguy, Lalique, Tiffany, Gaudin, Hohlwein, Saarinen, and many others. 288pp. 8⅜ x 11¼.
23515-7 Pa. $6.95

THE AMERICAN SENATOR, Anthony Trollope. Little known, long unavailable Trollope novel on a grand scale. Here are humorous comment on American vs. English culture, and stunning portrayal of a heroine/villainess. Superb evocation of Victorian village life. 561pp. 5⅜ x 8½.
23801-6 Pa. $6.00

WAS IT MURDER? James Hilton. The author of *Lost Horizon* and *Goodbye, Mr. Chips* wrote one detective novel (under a pen-name) which was quickly forgotten and virtually lost, even at the height of Hilton's fame. This edition brings it back—a finely crafted public school puzzle resplendent with Hilton's stylish atmosphere. A thoroughly English thriller by the creator of Shangri-la. 252pp. 5⅜ x 8. (Available in U.S. only)
23774-5 Pa. $3.00

CENTRAL PARK: A PHOTOGRAPHIC GUIDE, Victor Laredo and Henry Hope Reed. 121 superb photographs show dramatic views of Central Park: Bethesda Fountain, Cleopatra's Needle, Sheep Meadow, the Blockhouse, plus people engaged in many park activities: ice skating, bike riding, etc. Captions by former Curator of Central Park, Henry Hope Reed, provide historical view, changes, etc. Also photos of N.Y. landmarks on park's periphery. 96pp. 8½ x 11.
23750-8 Pa. $4.50

NANTUCKET IN THE NINETEENTH CENTURY, Clay Lancaster. 180 rare photographs, stereographs, maps, drawings and floor plans recreate unique American island society. Authentic scenes of shipwreck, lighthouses, streets, homes are arranged in geographic sequence to provide walking-tour guide to old Nantucket existing today. Introduction, captions. 160pp. 8⅞ x 11¾.
23747-8 Pa. $6.95

STONE AND MAN: A PHOTOGRAPHIC EXPLORATION, Andreas Feininger. 106 photographs by *Life* photographer Feininger portray man's deep passion for stone through the ages. Stonehenge-like megaliths, fortified towns, sculpted marble and crumbling tenements show textures, beauties, fascination. 128pp. 9¼ x 10¾.
23756-7 Pa. $5.95

CIRCLES, A MATHEMATICAL VIEW, D. Pedoe. Fundamental aspects of college geometry, non-Euclidean geometry, and other branches of mathematics: representing circle by point. Poincare model, isoperimetric property, etc. Stimulating recreational reading. 66 figures. 96pp. 5⅝ x 8¼.
63698-4 Pa. $2.75

THE DISCOVERY OF NEPTUNE, Morton Grosser. Dramatic scientific history of the investigations leading up to the actual discovery of the eighth planet of our solar system. Lucid, well-researched book by well-known historian of science. 172pp. 5⅜ x 8½.
23726-5 Pa. $3.00

THE DEVIL'S DICTIONARY. Ambrose Bierce. Barbed, bitter, brilliant witticisms in the form of a dictionary. Best, most ferocious satire America has produced. 145pp. 5⅜ x 8½.
20487-1 Pa. $1.75

HISTORY OF BACTERIOLOGY, William Bulloch. The only comprehensive history of bacteriology from the beginnings through the 19th century. Special emphasis is given to biography-Leeuwenhoek, etc. Brief accounts of 350 bacteriologists form a separate section. No clearer, fuller study, suitable to scientists and general readers, has yet been written. 52 illustrations. 448pp. 5⅝ x 8¼. 23761-3 Pa. $6.50

THE COMPLETE NONSENSE OF EDWARD LEAR, Edward Lear. All nonsense limericks, zany alphabets, Owl and Pussycat, songs, nonsense botany, etc., illustrated by Lear. Total of 321pp. 5⅜ x 8½. (Available in U.S. only) 20167-8 Pa. $3.00

INGENIOUS MATHEMATICAL PROBLEMS AND METHODS, Louis A. Graham. Sophisticated material from Graham *Dial*, applied and pure; stresses solution methods. Logic, number theory, networks, inversions, etc. 237pp. 5⅜ x 8½. 20545-2 Pa. $3.50

BEST MATHEMATICAL PUZZLES OF SAM LOYD, edited by Martin Gardner. Bizarre, original, whimsical puzzles by America's greatest puzzler. From fabulously rare *Cyclopedia*, including famous 14-15 puzzles, the Horse of a Different Color, 115 more. Elementary math. 150 illustrations. 167pp. 5⅜ x 8½. 20498-7 Pa. $2.50

THE BASIS OF COMBINATION IN CHESS, J. du Mont. Easy-to-follow, instructive book on elements of combination play, with chapters on each piece and every powerful combination team—two knights, bishop and knight, rook and bishop, etc. 250 diagrams. 218pp. 5⅜ x 8½. (Available in U.S. only) 23644-7 Pa. $3.50

MODERN CHESS STRATEGY, Ludek Pachman. The use of the queen, the active king, exchanges, pawn play, the center, weak squares, etc. Section on rook alone worth price of the book. Stress on the moderns. Often considered the most important book on strategy. 314pp. 5⅜ x 8½. 20290-9 Pa. $3.50

LASKER'S MANUAL OF CHESS, Dr. Emanuel Lasker. Great world champion offers very thorough coverage of all aspects of chess. Combinations, position play, openings, end game, aesthetics of chess, philosophy of struggle, much more. Filled with analyzed games. 390pp. 5⅜ x 8½. 20640-8 Pa. $4.00

500 MASTER GAMES OF CHESS, S. Tartakower, J. du Mont. Vast collection of great chess games from 1798-1938, with much material nowhere else readily available. Fully annotated, arranged by opening for easier study. 664pp. 5⅜ x 8½. 23208-5 Pa. $6.00

A GUIDE TO CHESS ENDINGS, Dr. Max Euwe, David Hooper. One of the finest modern works on chess endings. Thorough analysis of the most frequently encountered endings by former world champion. 331 examples, each with diagram. 248pp. 5⅜ x 8½. 23332-4 Pa. $3.50

SECOND PIATIGORSKY CUP, edited by Isaac Kashdan. One of the greatest tournament books ever produced in the English language. All 90 games of the 1966 tournament, annotated by players, most annotated by both players. Features Petrosian, Spassky, Fischer, Larsen, six others. 228pp. 5⅜ x 8½. 23572-6 Pa. $3.50

ENCYCLOPEDIA OF CARD TRICKS, revised and edited by Jean Hugard. How to perform over 600 card tricks, devised by the world's greatest magicians: impromptus, spelling tricks, key cards, using special packs, much, much more. Additional chapter on card technique. 66 illustrations. 402pp. 5⅜ x 8½. (Available in U.S. only) 21252-1 Pa. $3.95

MAGIC: STAGE ILLUSIONS, SPECIAL EFFECTS AND TRICK PHOTOGRAPHY, Albert A. Hopkins, Henry R. Evans. One of the great classics; fullest, most authorative explanation of vanishing lady, levitations, scores of other great stage effects. Also small magic, automata, stunts. 446 illustrations. 556pp. 5⅜ x 8½. 23344-8 Pa. $5.00

THE SECRETS OF HOUDINI, J. C. Cannell. Classic study of Houdini's incredible magic, exposing closely-kept professional secrets and revealing, in general terms, the whole art of stage magic. 67 illustrations. 279pp. 5⅜ x 8½. 22913-0 Pa. $3.00

HOFFMANN'S MODERN MAGIC, Professor Hoffmann. One of the best, and best-known, magicians' manuals of the past century. Hundreds of tricks from card tricks and simple sleight of hand to elaborate illusions involving construction of complicated machinery. 332 illustrations. 563pp. 5⅜ x 8½. 23623-4 Pa. $6.00

MADAME PRUNIER'S FISH COOKERY BOOK, Mme. S. B. Prunier. More than 1000 recipes from world famous Prunier's of Paris and London, specially adapted here for American kitchen. Grilled tournedos with anchovy butter, Lobster a la Bordelaise, Prunier's prized desserts, more. Glossary. 340pp. 5⅜ x 8½. (Available in U.S. only) 22679-4 Pa. $3.00

FRENCH COUNTRY COOKING FOR AMERICANS, Louis Diat. 500 easy-to-make, authentic provincial recipes compiled by former head chef at New York's Fitz-Carlton Hotel: onion soup, lamb stew, potato pie, more. 309pp. 5⅜ x 8½. 23665-X Pa. $3.95

SAUCES, FRENCH AND FAMOUS, Louis Diat. Complete book gives over 200 specific recipes: bechamel, Bordelaise, hollandaise, Cumberland, apricot, etc. Author was one of this century's finest chefs, originator of vichyssoise and many other dishes. Index. 156pp. 5⅜ x 8. 23663-3 Pa. $2.50

TOLL HOUSE TRIED AND TRUE RECIPES, Ruth Graves Wakefield. Authentic recipes from the famous Mass. restaurant: popovers, veal and ham loaf, Toll House baked beans, chocolate cake crumb pudding, much more. Many helpful hints. Nearly 700 recipes. Index. 376pp. 5⅜ x 8½. 23560-2 Pa. $4.00

"OSCAR" OF THE WALDORF'S COOKBOOK, Oscar Tschirky. Famous American chef reveals 3455 recipes that made Waldorf great; cream of French, German, American cooking, in all categories. Full instructions, easy home use. 1896 edition. 907pp. 6⅝ x 9⅜.   20790-0 Clothbd. $15.00

COOKING WITH BEER, Carole Fahy. Beer has as superb an effect on food as wine, and at fraction of cost. Over 250 recipes for appetizers, soups, main dishes, desserts, breads, etc. Index. 144pp. 5⅜ x 8½. (Available in U.S. only)
23661-7 Pa. $2.50

STEWS AND RAGOUTS, Kay Shaw Nelson. This international cookbook offers wide range of 108 recipes perfect for everyday, special occasions, meals-in-themselves, main dishes. Economical, nutritious, easy-to-prepare: goulash, Irish stew, boeuf bourguignon, etc. Index. 134pp. 5⅜ x 8½.
23662-5 Pa. $2.50

DELICIOUS MAIN COURSE DISHES, Marian Tracy. Main courses are the most important part of any meal. These 200 nutritious, economical recipes from around the world make every meal a delight. "I . . . have found it so useful in my own household,"—N.Y. Times. Index. 219pp. 5⅜ x 8½.
23664-1 Pa. $3.00

FIVE ACRES AND INDEPENDENCE, Maurice G. Kains. Great back-to-the-land classic explains basics of self-sufficient farming: economics, plants, crops, animals, orchards, soils, land selection, host of other necessary things. Do not confuse with skimpy faddist literature; Kains was one of America's greatest agriculturalists. 95 illustrations. 397pp. 5⅜ x 8½.
20974-1 Pa. $3.95

A PRACTICAL GUIDE FOR THE BEGINNING FARMER, Herbert Jacobs. Basic, extremely useful first book for anyone thinking about moving to the country and starting a farm. Simpler than Kains, with greater emphasis on country living in general. 246pp. 5⅜ x 8½.
23675-7 Pa. $3.50

A GARDEN OF PLEASANT FLOWERS (PARADISI IN SOLE: PARADISUS TERRESTRIS), John Parkinson. Complete, unabridged reprint of first (1629) edition of earliest great English book on gardens and gardening. More than 1000 plants & flowers of Elizabethan, Jacobean garden fully described, most with woodcut illustrations. Botanically very reliable, a "speaking garden" of exceeding charm. 812 illustrations. 628pp. 8½ x 12¼.
23392-8 Clothbd. $25.00

ACKERMANN'S COSTUME PLATES, Rudolph Ackermann. Selection of 96 plates from the Repository of Arts, best published source of costume for English fashion during the early 19th century. 12 plates also in color. Captions, glossary and introduction by editor Stella Blum. Total of 120pp. 8⅜ x 11¼.
23690-0 Pa. $4.50

MUSHROOMS, EDIBLE AND OTHERWISE, Miron E. Hard. Profusely illustrated, very useful guide to over 500 species of mushrooms growing in the Midwest and East. Nomenclature updated to 1976. 505 illustrations. 628pp. 6½ x 9¼. 23309-X Pa. $7.95

AN ILLUSTRATED FLORA OF THE NORTHERN UNITED STATES AND CANADA, Nathaniel L. Britton, Addison Brown. Encyclopedic work covers 4666 species, ferns on up. Everything. Full botanical information, illustration for each. This earlier edition is preferred by many to more recent revisions. 1913 edition. Over 4000 illustrations, total of 2087pp. 6⅛ x 9¼. 22642-5, 22643-3, 22644-1 Pa., Three-vol. set $24.00

MANUAL OF THE GRASSES OF THE UNITED STATES, A. S. Hitchcock, U.S. Dept. of Agriculture. The basic study of American grasses, both indigenous and escapes, cultivated and wild. Over 1400 species. Full descriptions, information. Over 1100 maps, illustrations. Total of 1051pp. 5⅜ x 8½. 22717-0, 22718-9 Pa., Two-vol. set $12.00

THE CACTACEAE,, Nathaniel L. Britton, John N. Rose. Exhaustive, definitive. Every cactus in the world. Full botanical descriptions. Thorough statement of nomenclatures, habitat, detailed finding keys. The one book needed by every cactus enthusiast. Over 1275 illustrations. Total of 1080pp. 8 x 10¼. 21191-6, 21192-4 Clothbd., Two-vol. set $35.00

AMERICAN MEDICINAL PLANTS, Charles F. Millspaugh. Full descriptions, 180 plants covered: history; physical description; methods of preparation with all chemical constituents extracted; all claimed curative or adverse effects. 180 full-page plates. Classification table. 804pp. 6½ x 9¼. 23034-1 Pa. $10.00

A MODERN HERBAL, Margaret Grieve. Much the fullest, most exact, most useful compilation of herbal material. Gigantic alphabetical encyclopedia, from aconite to zedoary, gives botanical information, medical properties, folklore, economic uses, and much else. Indispensable to serious reader. 161 illustrations. 888pp. 6½ x 9¼. (Available in U.S. only) 22798-7, 22799-5 Pa., Two-vol. set $11.00

THE HERBAL or GENERAL HISTORY OF PLANTS, John Gerard. The 1633 edition revised and enlarged by Thomas Johnson. Containing almost 2850 plant descriptions and 2705 superb illustrations, Gerard's Herbal is a monumental work, the book all modern English herbals are derived from, the one herbal every serious enthusiast should have in its entirety. Original editions are worth perhaps $750. 1678pp. 8½ x 12¼. 23147-X Clothbd. $50.00

MANUAL OF THE TREES OF NORTH AMERICA, Charles S. Sargent. The basic survey of every native tree and tree-like shrub, 717 species in all. Extremely full descriptions, information on habitat, growth, locales, economics, etc. Necessary to every serious tree lover. Over 100 finding keys. 783 illustrations. Total of 986pp. 5⅜ x 8½. 20277-1, 20278-X Pa., Two-vol. set $10.00

AMERICAN BIRD ENGRAVINGS, Alexander Wilson et al. All 76 plates. from Wilson's *American Ornithology* (1808-14), most important ornithological work before Audubon, plus 27 plates from the supplement (1825-33) by Charles Bonaparte. Over 250 birds portrayed. 8 plates also reproduced in full color. 111pp. 9⅜ x 12½. 23195-X Pa. $6.00

CRUICKSHANK'S PHOTOGRAPHS OF BIRDS OF AMERICA, Allan D. Cruickshank. Great ornithologist, photographer presents 177 closeups, groupings, panoramas, flightings, etc., of about 150 different birds. Expanded *Wings in the Wilderness*. Introduction by Helen G. Cruickshank. 191pp. 8¼ x 11. 23497-5 Pa. $6.00

AMERICAN WILDLIFE AND PLANTS, A. C. Martin, et al. Describes food habits of more than 1000 species of mammals, birds, fish. Special treatment of important food plants. Over 300 illustrations. 500pp. 5⅜ x 8½. 20793-5 Pa. $4.95

THE PEOPLE CALLED SHAKERS, Edward D. Andrews. Lifetime of research, definitive study of Shakers: origins, beliefs, practices, dances, social organization, furniture and crafts, impact on 19th-century USA, present heritage. Indispensable to student of American history, collector. 33 illustrations. 351pp. 5⅜ x 8½. 21081-2 Pa. $4.00

OLD NEW YORK IN EARLY PHOTOGRAPHS, Mary Black. New York City as it was in 1853-1901, through 196 wonderful photographs from N.-Y. Historical Society. Great Blizzard, Lincoln's funeral procession, great buildings. 228pp. 9 x 12. 22907-6 Pa. $7.95

MR. LINCOLN'S CAMERA MAN: MATHEW BRADY, Roy Meredith. Over 300 Brady photos reproduced directly from original negatives, photos. Jackson, Webster, Grant, Lee, Carnegie, Barnum; Lincoln; Battle Smoke, Death of Rebel Sniper, Atlanta Just After Capture. Lively commentary. 368pp. 8⅜ x 11¼. 23021-X Pa. $8.95

TRAVELS OF WILLIAM BARTRAM, William Bartram. From 1773-8, Bartram explored Northern Florida, Georgia, Carolinas, and reported on wild life, plants, Indians, early settlers. Basic account for period, entertaining reading. Edited by Mark Van Doren. 13 illustrations. 141pp. 5⅜ x 8½. 20013-2 Pa. $4.50

THE GENTLEMAN AND CABINET MAKER'S DIRECTOR, Thomas Chippendale. Full reprint, 1762 style book, most influential of all time; chairs, tables, sofas, mirrors, cabinets, etc. 200 plates, plus 24 photographs of surviving pieces. 249pp. 9⅞ x 12¾. 21601-2 Pa. $6.50

AMERICAN CARRIAGES, SLEIGHS, SULKIES AND CARTS, edited by Don H. Berkebile. 168 Victorian illustrations from catalogues, trade journals, fully captioned. Useful for artists. Author is Assoc. Curator, Div. of Transportation of Smithsonian Institution. 168pp. 8½ x 9½. 23328-6 Pa. $5.00

THE SENSE OF BEAUTY, George Santayana. Masterfully written discussion of nature of beauty, materials of beauty, form, expression; art, literature, social sciences all involved. 168pp. 5⅜ x 8½.   20238-0 Pa. $2.50

ON THE IMPROVEMENT OF THE UNDERSTANDING, Benedict Spinoza. Also contains *Ethics, Correspondence,* all in excellent R. Elwes translation. Basic works on entry to philosophy, pantheism, exchange of ideas with great contemporaries. 402pp. 5⅜ x 8½.   20250-X Pa. $4.50

THE TRAGIC SENSE OF LIFE, Miguel de Unamuno. Acknowledged masterpiece of existential literature, one of most important books of 20th century. Introduction by Madariaga. 367pp. 5⅜ x 8½.

20257-7 Pa. $3.50

THE GUIDE FOR THE PERPLEXED, Moses Maimonides. Great classic of medieval Judaism attempts to reconcile revealed religion (Pentateuch, commentaries) with Aristotelian philosophy. Important historically, still relevant in problems. Unabridged Friedlander translation. Total of 473pp. 5⅜ x 8½.   20351-4 Pa. $5.00

THE I CHING (THE BOOK OF CHANGES), translated by James Legge. Complete translation of basic text plus appendices by Confucius, and Chinese commentary of most penetrating divination manual ever prepared. Indispensable to study of early Oriental civilizations, to modern inquiring reader. 448pp. 5⅜ x 8½.   21062-6 Pa. $4.00

THE EGYPTIAN BOOK OF THE DEAD, E. A. Wallis Budge. Complete reproduction of Ani's papyrus, finest ever found. Full hieroglyphic text, interlinear transliteration, word for word translation, smooth translation. Basic work, for Egyptology, for modern study of psychic matters. Total of 533pp. 6½ x 9¼. (Available in U.S. only)   21866-X Pa. $4.95

THE GODS OF THE EGYPTIANS, E. A. Wallis Budge. Never excelled for richness, fullness: all gods, goddesses, demons, mythical figures of Ancient Egypt; their legends, rites, incarnations, variations, powers, etc. Many hieroglyphic texts cited. Over 225 illustrations, plus 6 color plates. Total of 988pp. 6⅛ x 9¼. (Available in U.S. only)

22055-9, 22056-7 Pa., Two-vol. set $12.00

THE ENGLISH AND SCOTTISH POPULAR BALLADS, Francis J. Child. Monumental, still unsuperseded; all known variants of Child ballads, commentary on origins, literary references, Continental parallels, other features. Added: papers by G. L. Kittredge, W. M. Hart. Total of 2761pp. 6½ x 9¼.

21409-5, 21410-9, 21411-7, 21412-5, 21413-3 Pa., Five-vol. set $37.50

CORAL GARDENS AND THEIR MAGIC, Bronsilaw Malinowski. Classic study of the methods of tilling the soil and of agricultural rites in the Trobriand Islands of Melanesia. Author is one of the most important figures in the field of modern social anthropology. 143 illustrations. Indexes. Total of 911pp. of text. 5⅝ x 8¼. (Available in U.S. only)

23597-1 Pa. $12.95

THE PHILOSOPHY OF HISTORY, Georg W. Hegel. Great classic of Western thought develops concept that history is not chance but a rational process, the evolution of freedom. 457pp. 5⅜ x 8½. 20112-0 Pa. $4.50

LANGUAGE, TRUTH AND LOGIC, Alfred J. Ayer. Famous, clear introduction to Vienna, Cambridge schools of Logical Positivism. Role of philosophy, elimination of metaphysics, nature of analysis, etc. 160pp. 5⅜ x 8½. (Available in U.S. only) 20010-8 Pa. $1.75

A PREFACE TO LOGIC, Morris R. Cohen. Great City College teacher in renowned, easily followed exposition of formal logic, probability, values, logic and world order and similar topics; no previous background needed. 209pp. 5⅜ x 8½. 23517-3 Pa. $3.50

REASON AND NATURE, Morris R. Cohen. Brilliant analysis of reason and its multitudinous ramifications by charismatic teacher. Interdisciplinary, synthesizing work widely praised when it first appeared in 1931. Second (1953) edition. Indexes. 496pp. 5⅜ x 8½. 23633-1 Pa. $6.00

AN ESSAY CONCERNING HUMAN UNDERSTANDING, John Locke. The only complete edition of enormously important classic, with authoritative editorial material by A. C. Fraser. Total of 1176pp. 5⅜ x 8½. 20530-4, 20531-2 Pa., Two-vol. set $14.00

HANDBOOK OF MATHEMATICAL FUNCTIONS WITH FORMULAS, GRAPHS, AND MATHEMATICAL TABLES, edited by Milton Abramowitz and Irene A. Stegun. Vast compendium: 29 sets of tables, some to as high as 20 places. 1,046pp. 8 x 10½. 61272-4 Pa. $14.95

MATHEMATICS FOR THE PHYSICAL SCIENCES, Herbert S. Wilf. Highly acclaimed work offers clear presentations of vector spaces and matrices, orthogonal functions, roots of polynomial equations, conformal mapping, calculus of variations, etc. Knowledge of theory of functions of real and complex variables is assumed. Exercises and solutions. Index. 284pp. 5⅝ x 8¼. 63635-6 Pa. $4.50

THE PRINCIPLE OF RELATIVITY, Albert Einstein et al. Eleven most important original papers on special and general theories. Seven by Einstein, two by Lorentz, one each by Minkowski and Weyl. All translated, unabridged. 216pp. 5⅜ x 8½. 60081-5 Pa. $3.00

THERMODYNAMICS, Enrico Fermi. A classic of modern science. Clear, organized treatment of systems, first and second laws, entropy, thermodynamic potentials, gaseous reactions, dilute solutions, entropy constant. No math beyond calculus required. Problems. 160pp. 5⅜ x 8½. 60361-X Pa. $2.75

ELEMENTARY MECHANICS OF FLUIDS, Hunter Rouse. Classic undergraduate text widely considered to be far better than many later books. Ranges from fluid velocity and acceleration to role of compressibility in fluid motion. Numerous examples, questions, problems. 224 illustrations. 376pp. 5⅝ x 8¼. 63699-2 Pa. $5.00

AN AUTOBIOGRAPHY, Margaret Sanger. Exciting personal account of hard-fought battle for woman's right to birth control, against prejudice, church, law. Foremost feminist document. 504pp. 5⅜ x 8½.

20470-7 Pa. $5.50

MY BONDAGE AND MY FREEDOM, Frederick Douglass. Born as a slave, Douglass became outspoken force in antislavery movement. The best of Douglass's autobiographies. Graphic description of slave life. Introduction by P. Foner. 464pp. 5⅜ x 8½.

22457-0 Pa. $5.00

LIVING MY LIFE, Emma Goldman. Candid, no holds barred account by foremost American anarchist: her own life, anarchist movement, famous contemporaries, ideas and their impact. Struggles and confrontations in America, plus deportation to U.S.S.R. Shocking inside account of persecution of anarchists under Lenin. 13 plates. Total of 944pp. 5⅜ x 8½.

22543-7, 22544-5 Pa., Two-vol. set $9.00

LETTERS AND NOTES ON THE MANNERS, CUSTOMS AND CONDITIONS OF THE NORTH AMERICAN INDIANS, George Catlin. Classic account of life among Plains Indians: ceremonies, hunt, warfare, etc. Dover edition reproduces for first time all original paintings. 312 plates. 572pp. of text. 6⅛ x 9¼.

22118-0, 22119-9 Pa.. Two-vol. set $10.00

THE MAYA AND THEIR NEIGHBORS, edited by Clarence L. Hay, others. Synoptic view of Maya civilization in broadest sense, together with Northern, Southern neighbors. Integrates much background, valuable detail not elsewhere. Prepared by greatest scholars: Kroeber, Morley, Thompson, Spinden, Vaillant, many others. Sometimes called Tozzer Memorial Volume. 60 illustrations, linguistic map. 634pp. 5⅜ x 8½.

23510-6 Pa. $7.50

HANDBOOK OF THE INDIANS OF CALIFORNIA, A. L. Kroeber. Foremost American anthropologist offers complete ethnographic study of each group. Monumental classic. 459 illustrations, maps. 995pp. 5⅜ x 8½.

23368-5 Pa. $10.00

SHAKTI AND SHAKTA, Arthur Avalon. First book to give clear, cohesive analysis of Shakta doctrine, Shakta ritual and Kundalini Shakti (yoga). Important work by one of world's foremost students of Shaktic and Tantric thought. 732pp. 5⅜ x 8½. (Available in U.S. only)

23645-5 Pa. $7.95

AN INTRODUCTION TO THE STUDY OF THE MAYA HIEROGLYPHS, Syvanus Griswold Morley. Classic study by one of the truly great figures in hieroglyph research. Still the best introduction for the student for reading Maya hieroglyphs. New introduction by J. Eric S. Thompson. 117 illustrations. 284pp. 5⅜ x 8½.

23108-9 Pa. $4.00

A STUDY OF MAYA ART, Herbert J. Spinden. Landmark classic interprets Maya symbolism, estimates styles, covers ceramics, architecture, murals, stone carvings as artforms. Still a basic book in area. New introduction by J. Eric Thompson. Over 750 illustrations. 341pp. 8⅜ x 11¼.

21235-1 Pa. $6.95

THE STANDARD BOOK OF QUILT MAKING AND COLLECTING, Marguerite Ickis. Full information, full-sized patterns for making 46 traditional quilts, also 150 other patterns. Quilted cloths, lame, satin quilts, etc. 483 illustrations. 273pp. 6⅞ x 9⅝.   20582-7 Pa. $4.50

ENCYCLOPEDIA OF VICTORIAN NEEDLEWORK, S. Caulfield, Blanche Saward. Simply inexhaustible gigantic alphabetical coverage of every traditional needlecraft—stitches, materials, methods, tools, types of work; definitions, many projects to be made. 1200 illustrations; double-columned text. 697pp. 8⅛ x 11.   22800-2, 22801-0 Pa., Two-vol. set $12.00

MECHANICK EXERCISES ON THE WHOLE ART OF PRINTING, Joseph Moxon. First complete book (1683-4) ever written about typography, a compendium of everything known about printing at the latter part of 17th century. Reprint of 2nd (1962) Oxford Univ. Press edition. 74 illustrations. Total of 550pp. 6⅛ x 9¼.   23617-X Pa. $7.95

PAPERMAKING, Dard Hunter. Definitive book on the subject by the foremost authority in the field. Chapters dealing with every aspect of history of craft in every part of the world. Over 320 illustrations. 2nd, revised and enlarged (1947) edition. 672pp. 5⅜ x 8½.   23619-6 Pa. $7.95

THE ART DECO STYLE, edited by Theodore Menten. Furniture, jewelry, metalwork, ceramics, fabrics, lighting fixtures, interior decors, exteriors, graphics from pure French sources. Best sampling around. Over 400 photographs. 183pp. 8⅜ x 11¼.   22824-X Pa. $5.00

Prices subject to change without notice.

Available at your book dealer or write for free catalogue to Dept. GI, Dover Publications, Inc., 180 Varick St., N.Y., N.Y. 10014. Dover publishes more than 175 books each year on science, elementary and advanced mathematics, biology, music, art, literary history, social sciences and other areas.